EYES ON JESUS

A 90-Day Discernment Devotional

TIM FERRARA

Vide Press
P.O. Box 1264, Warrenton, VA 20188

ISBN: 978-1-954618-30-5 (Print)

Printed in the United States of America

Dedication

*This book is dedicated to my beautiful wife and
best friend, Jamie, who always helps me keep
my eyes on Jesus each and every day*

Do you ever feel helpless? Hopeless? Like your life is falling apart with no end in sight? Like the waves of this world are crashing against you and God is nowhere to be found? Maybe you feel that way right now. If we are honest with ourselves, sometimes it is our own poor decisions that lead us down a path of trouble and heartache. Other times, trials blindside us from no fault of our own. In both instances, we need to keep our eyes on Jesus to either get back on the right path or to stay the course.

The first book I wrote is called *Everyday Discernment: The Importance of Spirit-Led Decision Making.* The reason I felt like God wanted me to write that book is because of the importance that discernment is to our daily life and the decisions we make that can either honor God or not. I define discernment as Spirit-infused decision making. Discernment is a skill that grows over time as we learn and get closer to Jesus. Think of discernment like a spiritual muscle that we can choose to use to overcome obstacles, or we can choose to let the muscle get weak and be untrained.

We can attain discernment through three sources. The Bible, the Holy Spirit, and godly relationships. The Bible is our foundation as Christians, our bedrock. The Bible is the never changing, infallible Word of God and is just as relevant and valuable today as it was in the past. The Bible is under attack and we live in a culture and world that either wants to destroy it completely or wants to relegate it to a "good book" written by men who were not inspired by God. The Bible is rich with wisdom and no matter if you have read it once or a thousand times, there is always something more to be learned. The Bible is living and active, sharper than any double-edged sword (Heb. 4:12).

We can also discern with the help of the Holy Spirit, who is our comforter and source of truth. The Holy Spirit can quicken something to you in an instant if you are listening to Him. We make thousands of decisions daily and if you are leaning into help from God, He will quicken to you in a moment when you need it which path to take. The Bible gives a foundation of how to live and who God is, but it doesn't tell you who to marry or what job to take or where to live. The Holy Spirit guides us through life and leads us.

The final source of discernment is godly relationships. There is wisdom is the counsel of others and not just any relationship but ones where God is living and active in their lives as well. God will reveal truth to us in others if we are humble and realize we do not have all the answers. Others in life have wisdom because of years and others because of relationship with God and with you. God gives us spouses, friends, pastors, mentors, and even children to speak truth to us.

Making decisions that honor God is not just in the large decisions that need times of fasting and prayer. I outline in my first book many areas of our life where we need discernment each and every day. Areas like finances, how we use our time, how we avoid sin, relationships, finances, parenting, marriage, entertainment media, and even social media usage. Making a good decision in the past does not guarantee a good decision today, which is why we need Jesus each and every day.

God was moving in my heart for this concept of keeping our eyes on Jesus. I started using the hashtag "eyesonJesus" in my social media posts and I would end my podcast episodes by saying, "Until next week, go with God, grow in discernment, and keep your eyes on Jesus." Then I started writing short blogs, if you will, or concepts relating to discernment and what it means to keep our eyes on Jesus every day. This led to a fourteen-day devotional and now the ninety-day version which you are reading now.

If we don't keep our eyes on Jesus, they are on something else. Peter walked on water ... until he took his eyes off Jesus. I believe that there are enough distractions in this life that the Enemy uses to keep us focused on anything but Jesus. Keeping our eyes on Jesus is not a one-time thing where we commit to it and then we are good for months on end. No, we need a daily walk with Christ, even if we don't "feel" like it. Feelings are a terrible source of discernment.

I really tried to be Holy Spirit led as I wrote this. I took my time. I did not write more than one devotional a day. I waited and did not write for days until I had a fresh inspiration on what to write. Many of the examples I mention in this devotional are examples in my life that I have not thought about for years, but I give God the credit for quickening these to me and helping me relate them to Scripture and practical application. I genuinely believe this final devotional contains the message God wanted me to share and I pray it draws you closer to Jesus as you read it.

My guess is that you have read a devotional before. If you are like me, you have read devotionals with different methods over the years. Some devotionals I would casually read, some I would start and then give up on, others I would read, reflect, and journal as I went through it.

We are called to not just be hearers of the Word but doers (James 1:22). This devotional is designed for self-reflection, to not just read a nice or funny commentary on a Bible verse but to be Holy Spirit led yourself on what God is wanting to show you each and every day you read it.

How you read this devotional is between you and God, but I would recommend that you read no more than one day at a time. Maybe you will want to read the daily Bible verse in the context of the rest of the chapter where it is found. There is space for you to answer the reflection questions at the end of every day. Sure, you could skip them, but I will challenge you to write down your answers. If you decide to reread this devotional after the ninety days are over (which is a great idea by the way), you can look back at what you wrote and then write more about what God did in your life since you first read it.

My prayer is that this devotional helps incorporate skills and wisdom into your life that make it easier to keep your eyes on Jesus daily. I pray that you grow in discernment, so that you can make better daily decisions that honor God. I pray that you will be able to discern against distraction and the lies of the enemy. I pray that you find or recommit your identity and calling in Jesus and that you pursue Him with a new boldness and passion than ever before!

--- *Day 1* ---

> *"Therefore, since we are surrounded by such a great cloud of witnesses, let us throw off everything that hinders and the sin that so easily entangles. And let us run with perseverance the race marked out for us, fixing your eyes on Jesus, the pioneer and perfecter of faith."*
>
> HEBREWS 12:1-2A (NIV)

In crisis, you may see first responders or have been a part of a situation that requires the survivor being saved to keep their eyes on their rescuer. If a survivor is being pulled out of a burning building or a wrecked car, it's important to keep the survivor calm and keep their eyes on the professional giving the instructions so that they do not get overwhelmed with the situation and start to panic. If the survivor panics, there is a good chance they will not follow the instructions that keep them alive. The survivor is not oblivious to the danger; however, they don't let the danger overwhelm them when they are focused on escaping it.

[handwritten] Paramount

As Christians, we are called in Hebrews to keep our eyes fixed on Jesus as we run the Christian race. If the writer of Hebrews is talking to Christians, should not it be obvious that Jesus is our focus? Well, not necessarily. We are easily distracted by the cares of this world and when problems arise or crisis hits, it's easy to be overwhelmed by the situation.

Having our eyes fixed on Jesus during the good times will build our foundation on the Rock of our salvation. Having our eyes fixed on Jesus during the bad times will allow us to find peace and hope when the world around us is stealing both of those things.

Jesus called Peter out of the boat to walk on water and everything was fine until Peter took his eyes off Jesus. He focused on the wind and the waves instead of the Lord. It is much easier to focus on Jesus when things are going well and we have food, good health, and blessings.

Having discernment in our decisions requires us to keep our eyes fixed on Jesus. Decisions are easier and aligned with the will of God and the truth of the Bible when we don't lose sight of this simple, yet not to be overlooked, fact in the Christian race. You will not make great decisions that honor God when your eyes are not fixed on Jesus and His Word.

REFLECT: How have you taken your eyes off Jesus recently? What ways can you commit to today to stay focused on keeping Jesus first in your decision making?

*"Do not be conformed to this world, but be transformed
by the renewal of your mind, that by testing you may
discern what is the will of God, what is good and
acceptable and perfect."*
ROMANS 12:2 (ESV)

What do you think of when you hear the word "transformed?" For me, I think of Superman. You know, the Clark Kent running into a phone booth and poof! He is instantly transformed into Superman, ready to beat up a bad guy and save the damsel in distress.

However, transformation does not have to be instantaneous. It can be a process, taking seconds or even a lifetime. As Christians, once we receive salvation, we have the Holy Spirit inside of us that transforms us and gives us the mind of Christ and the same Spirit that raised Christ from the dead. However, the rest of our life, after salvation, is a process we call sanctification. Sanctification is a life-long process of pursuing perfection, as Jesus is perfect, while knowing we will never obtain perfection.

So why pursue a goal if you know you will never achieve it? Seems pointless, right? Well, no it's not... That is like saying, what is the point of graduating kindergarten when you know they are not ready for college? As Christians, we should be able to look back on our life and see growth over time.

The Christian transformation is, or should be, more like a caterpillar to a butterfly. The old has gone and the new has come as 2 Corinthians 5:7 tells us which is also interesting because the Greek word Paul used in Romans 12:2 for transform, literally means metamorphosis! It's a process to get there, but there is beauty and freedom on the other side. We should look nothing like our old self and the sooner we can get there the better it will be for our peace and relationship with Jesus.

To discern the will of God we need to renew our minds, we cannot make decisions that honor God if we are still thinking with our sin nature or with influences of the world. We have to put to death the sin which so easily ensnares (Col. 3:5) and be transformed into thinking like Jesus.

REFLECT: In what ways have you transformed your mind to be more like Jesus and not the world? What areas are you still working on? Pray to God about them.

Day 3

"And if the Spirit of him who raised Jesus from the dead is living in you, he who raised Christ from the dead will also give life to your mortal bodies because of his Spirit who lives in you."
ROMANS 8:11 (NIV)

I am fascinated by this verse. I have found myself thinking about it a lot. Too often I would skim right past it without ever fully trying to understand it. Whenever I would try to contemplate it, I realized that I cannot fully grasp what is trying to be conveyed here even though I believe it in faith.

The same Spirit that was there hovering over the waters at creation, there at the burning bush with Moses and parting the Red Sea, there when David killed Goliath, there when Elijah was taken to heaven in a fiery chariot has been interwoven through every story in all of history!

I believe I have the Spirit of God as a gift given to those who are redeemed. There is fruit of the Spirit that should be displayed in my life. I can pray in the Spirit and live by the Spirit. This is the same Spirit that raised Christ from the dead! How does that exactly work with my spirit relating to God's spirit, how does He live in me, how does it all function when some Christians don't move in the Spirit? It can cause my head to hurt!

We are in no way gods and will not become gods, but we should have the mind of Christ because we have the Holy Spirit. This verse in Romans is not talking about the resurrection when we will be raised to life and receive new bodies at the end of days. This verse is talking about NOW, His Spirit that lives in us right now.

The conclusion along this line of thinking relating to discernment is knowing that, if we have the mind of Christ now and the Spirit inside of us, we should be making decisions along the narrow path. This is not to say we won't be tempted by alluring options in our path to discernment, but if we are aligned with the Spirit, the best option will be made known to us.

We have all the Holy Spirit available to us, but the Holy Spirit does not always have all of us. Meaning that we need to be in communion with Him and listen to what He has to say without always relying on our own strength.

REFLECT: What is the significance to you of having the same Spirit in you that raised Christ from the dead? How should this impact your life on a daily basis? List some areas of your life where you could rely more on the Holy Spirit for discernment.

Day 4

*"The person without the Spirit does not accept the
things that come from the Spirit of God but considers
them foolishness, and cannot understand them because
they are discerned only through the Spirit."*
1 CORINTHIANS 2:14 (NIV)

Did you ever look ahead in school at the math books of future
grades? Maybe a sibling brought home their books and you
glanced through them thinking, "I'm never going to understand
this stuff!" Maybe you looked ahead at a college entrance exam
five to ten years before you were ready to take it.

It becomes evident that once you learn the rules of math
(or any subject), practice, listen to the teacher, and progress
at the right pace the later material that looked so hard,
actually wasn't as bad as it seemed (regardless if you like
the subject or not).

The Holy Spirit brings revelation and is a source of our
discernment as Christians. God is constantly training us,
growing us, showing us new things so that when we make
progress toward sanctification, we should be able to look
back and see how far we've grown. Ten years ago, we may
have never seen ourselves being the followers of Christ
that we are now. Conversely, if you are not further along
in your Christian race, it might be time for reflection and

discipleship. We should keep pursuing our Father as He always has more to reveal.

"When the Spirit illuminates the heart, then a part of the man sees which never saw before; a part of him knows which never knew before, and that with a kind of knowing which the most acute thinker cannot imitate." A.W. Tozer

If you are like me you need to read some of Tozer's writings a few times to grasp what he is trying to convey, so read that again if your brain just glossed over it.

Just like in math, if we are obedient to the rules (the Bible), listen to the teacher (Holy Spirit), practice (read the Bible), and progress at the right pace (understand where you are at in the Christian race and have grace for those who are in different stages than you), then we will be able to discern much more than we would have in our own earthly knowledge.

We cannot compare our walk with God to someone else's! This is crucial to understand for multiple reasons. What we see publicly from someone else may not be who they are in private. Also, we do not always see the journey they have been on and the things they overcame to get there.

REFLECT: How can you pray that your relationship with God advances over the next few years? What does that look like in practical steps (ex: Bible reading, less sin, more vibrant prayer life, etc.?) Pray a humble prayer asking God to help you grow with Him.

 Day 5

"Let us not become weary in doing good, for at the
proper time we will reap a harvest if we do not give up."
GALATIANS 6:9 (NIV)

There's a lot of farming analogies in the Bible and unless
you are proficient in agriculture, it can be lost in translation.
I can understand what Paul is trying to say here but for the
culture at the time, this was their life and livelihood!

Farmers put a lot of time and effort into planting and
cultivating a crop for an eventual reward, the harvest. The
harvest not only fed their families but also allowed for
them to pay for everything else, as well as support the local
community, and be able to invest in future crops.

I think of the Little House on the Prairie series I used to watch
as a kid. Pa would spend time planting but then he might get
hurt, there would be a tornado, a frost, a storm, or any number
of other tragedies that would make for a good episode. If
a crop was lost, it was devastating to the family. The blood,
sweat, and tears put into seeing the crop to harvest were all
worth the effort because it meant food on the table.

It's easy to think in our microwave culture that if I don't
see the immediate results of my good actions (like tithing,
being faithful, avoiding sin, or loving my neighbor) that

they won't come. However, God promises that the last will be first and the first will be last. We have an eternal reward but also earthly blessings if we follow God in obedience. We must remember to not make the blessing our focus, instead, focus on keeping our eyes on Jesus!

It's important for us as Christians to remember that we don't always reap in the same season we sow. Our verse in Galatians reminds us to not get tired of doing good. It can be easy to get burned out, especially if you work in ministry or volunteer. Our flesh can get tired of doing good. We need to be strengthened by the Spirit of God daily.

There are also consequences for sin; we will reap what we sow when it comes to unrepentant sin. Everything that is in the dark will be brought to light the Bible says (Luke 12:2). Even if it looks like we "got away" with something, we really didn't. God sees all and even though grace can cover our salvation, it doesn't prevent earthly consequences from our stupid mistakes. This is why keeping your eyes on Jesus and discernment are so important!

REFLECT: What am I sowing now into my life and those around me? What is the future harvest that I can expect from my actions today?

Day 6

"The heart of the discerning acquires knowledge, for the ears of the wise seek it out."
PROVERBS 18:15 (NIV)

Remember researching for a school paper? For some it's remembering further back than others. I even remember going to a physical library and using the Dewey Decimal System. Wow, that's old! No matter what the subject, if you wanted to write a paper worthy of a good grade, you needed to do your research.

Many times, the subject was unfamiliar to me, so I had to really make sure that I was thorough in my research. I still remember my favorite paper in high school about the Loch Ness Monster. It created a desire in me to someday see the famous loch in Scotland.

Now imagine if you put together a research paper in an hour using fancy words with no real substance, you didn't cite any meaningful sources, you did not follow the basic formatting rules, and you even plagiarized someone else. It would certainly fail!

Faith is enough for salvation, but it is not always enough when making decisions, we have to do our research! When we make decisions as Christians, we cannot rely on our own knowledge but God's. Gathering knowledge transpires, primarily, in understanding the Bible. The Holy Spirit can quicken discernment in a second, but most major decisions require prayer, biblical application, advice from godly people in your life, time, and more prayer!

It's easier to make a good decision when you take the urgency of the moment out of the equation.

Sins are often due to a lack of research and forethought. Many sins are done in the spur of the moment, without ever contemplating the actions fully. We give in to the desires of the flesh and many times regret our decision. Consider anger, lust, envy, jealously, and even something as serious as murder is often done in the passion of the moment.

As a culture we like fast decisions, even in leadership training they will tell you a good leader can make decisions on their feet with minimal thought. This can be a great leadership quality but as Christians, sometimes we need to wait on the Lord and renew our strength as Isaiah 40:31 teaches us.

REFLECT: What is a decision that you made in haste that you should have taken more time to pray about? What do you need to be patient and wait on the Lord for today?

_____

_____

_____

_____

_____

Day 7

"Who is wise? Let them realize these things. Who is discerning? Let them understand. The ways of the Lord are right; the righteous walk in them but the rebellious stumble in them."
HOSEA 14:9 (NIV)

I would go hiking a lot during my childhood and there were many trails on the mountain I would frequently visit. There were easier trails than others and they were marked with difficulty markers. One path in particular was the most challenging, but it took you to the top of the mountain and allowed you to see over the whole valley in a beautiful landscape. I witnessed many start on this path but only go so far and turn back.

There are a lot of parallels with the Christian journey and hiking, just read *Pilgrim's Progress*. Jesus called following Him the "narrow road." Many will not make it to the end of the path that goes to the Father. Many start on the right path only to abandon it. Some go along easier paths, not wanting to be challenged at all. And some just stay at home altogether, allowing apathy to overcome them.

Jesus never promised that the journey would be easy, but He did promise it would be worth it. There are hills and valleys in our path, good times and bad. What is important is that we do not give up. We should rely on those who have walked the path before and have the wisdom of the trails, like our pastors, elders, teachers, etc.

The rebellious Christians stumble on the right path because they want it to be easy! They think that they are on the wrong path because of the trials that await them instead of persevering and being obedient to the Word of God.

Discernment will cause us to make the right decisions even if they are not easy and even if there is no immediate reward in making them. If we take the option off the table of quitting or following another path, then there is no other choice than to persevere and make it up the narrow road!

REFLECT: Do I find joy in the things of God or are they a stumbling block to me? Am I committed to the narrow path regardless of the obstacle? Pray for strength as you travel down the narrow path.

Day 8

"But if we were more discerning with regard to
ourselves, we would not come under such judgment."
1 CORINTHIANS 11:31 (NIV)

I used to play basketball regularly. In pickup games you would be your own referee and call out when you got fouled. There's always that one player who calls a foul when he gets slightly tapped and yet he is very defensive when he gets a blatant foul called against him! This situation alone caused more arguments and fights on the court than any other reason during the time I played.

Playing with or against defensive and aggressive players can be frustrating. They are only thinking of themselves and not trying to win the game by being a good sport and having fun.

We can be very defensive as Christians, often thinking that nothing is wrong with us, but "oh let me tell you what so and so is doing wrong!" This is gossip and it is uncalled for in the body of Christ. Jesus made this truly clear when He preached to worry about the log in your own eye before looking at the speck in your brother's.

The answer as to why we don't want to self-reflect is simple — we don't want to uncover what we find, and we definitely don't want to change. We want others to change but don't always lead the way. Have you had the boss that tells you to do something but won't do the same thing being asked of you? It's frustrating. We must realize that we are an example to those in our sphere of influence. Our co-workers, children, spouse, unbelievers, and Christians are all watching our life which is supposed to be a testimony that points others to Jesus.

Paul is referring to partaking in communion in 1 Corinthians 11:31. But discernment starts not just with decisions we make but internal reflection. If we focus on what is happening internally and get our heart and mind right, then the decisions we end up making will flow from a place of truth in our identity in Christ.

It's never too late to change, it just becomes a lot harder when you get set in your ways and hardened by life experiences.

REFLECT: How have you been defensive when someone brought truth to you? How can you incorporate a time of self-reflection in your quiet time with God? Who can speak truth and wisdom in your life that you can rely on?

_____

_____

_____

_____

_____

_____

_____

Day 9

"And this is my prayer: that your love may abound more and more in knowledge and depth of insight, so that you may be able to discern what is best and may be pure and blameless for the day of Christ, filled with the fruit of righteousness that comes through Jesus Christ."
PHILIPPIANS 1:9-10 (NIV)

Think of a time you made a poor decision... maybe it was a bad choice for a girlfriend or boyfriend, maybe it was a poor business deal or a career choice, or maybe it was a negative comment you made that hurt someone's feelings. Whatever the poor decision you made was, you couldn't see the results of that decision and the regret you would feel later. That's why they say hindsight is 20/20 because we see back at the past with improved clarity of what we did wrong or what we did right.

If you could go back and stop yourself from making a bad decision you probably would. However, we need bad decisions to know what good decisions look like. It is a part of the growth process; we have all made, and will continue to make, poor decisions. The trick is not making the same mistake twice and growing in our discernment.

God is not confined to time, so He sees all decisions in perfect clarity with the past, present, and future in parallel with each other. We should trust in God and His plan for our life through the Bible and we should ask for wisdom from the Holy Spirit to help us avoid pitfalls along the way.

In the verse above, Paul prays that the Philippians' love would abound in knowledge and depth of insight so that they would discern... but what's love got to do with it?

Paul was referring to love here as unity among the body of Christ. As we display love, we understand more of God because God is love. There are many examples in the Bible on how we should be an example in loving others not to mention Jesus who said to love the Lord with all your heart and love your neighbor as yourself.

But this verse as it relates to discernment is remarkably interesting because as we love and grow in knowledge, we will be able to discern clearly. How is love and discernment related? To make this clearer, think about the other extreme — what good decisions did you make that were done in hate? Probably not many, if any...

REFLECT: How do I show the love of Christ to others during my daily routines? How can I make decisions through the lens of God's love for me?

"But solid food is for the mature, who because of practice have their senses trained to discern good and evil."
HEBREWS 5:14 (NIV)

One of my favorite skits on a show called *Mad TV* was about this giant man-baby named Stuart. He would act like a three-year-old even though he was obviously a middle-aged man. It sounds stupid and it probably is if I tried watching it again, but the concept of someone who never aged makes for comedic situations. There's also viral videos or stories on social media once in a while of parents who still pamper their grown kids; ten-year olds still on a bottle, moms who chew up their kid's food like a momma bird then spit it out, etc. All of these go against the normal maturity you come to expect in raising kids.

Imagine if your kids were born and then they had to fend for themselves without the first 0-18 years of equipping, maturing, and training? It would be tragic.

The writer of Hebrews explains the concept of maturing in believers as solid food and milk. Just as one would expect a child to mature over time, so Christians should be maturing over the years after salvation. If you look back ten years into your Christian walk, you should see a maturing in the decisions you are making, the resistance to sin, a more abundant prayer life, daily reading of the Word of God, etc.

The journey to maturity as a Christian will never be completed and much failure will be involved. Hebrews says "because of practice" you can train to discern between good and evil. Practice makes perfect but practice also allows for failure. Think of practicing basketball shots. If you shoot a hundred shots, you may miss half of them. But over time, maybe you miss 40, then 30, then 20, etc. Even professional players will not make all 100 shots.

We must learn from failure as Christians. We can make better decisions and grow in discernment as we are open to the process of maturing in our walk with Jesus Christ.

We don't want to be a spiritual baby, decades into our walk with Christ and still not able to digest the meat of the Word of God or the deeper things that God can show us. There is always a next level in our faith that God is willing to take us, but we have to graduate and move on from where we are at.

REFLECT: What areas of my Christian life have I matured in over the last few years? What areas do I still need to mature in?

_____

_____

_____

_____

_____

Day 11

"Suppose one of you wants to build a tower. Won't you first sit down and estimate the cost to see if you have enough money to complete it?"
LUKE 14:28 (NIV)

Jesus told this example in the context of becoming His disciple, no, not as one of His 12, but as a lifelong, committed follower. He wants us to count the cost ahead of time so that we know what we are getting into, so that there are no tricks being played.

Imagine if you met someone you liked and the very next day you eloped (yes, I know this happens). Wisdom would say that this is not the foundation for a long relationship. You don't know much about this person that you are committing your life to, you don't know if you will be compatible in your goals, beliefs, finances, personalities, or family dynamics. This is why most people date in order to know if they will be compatible for marriage. If you have been married for many years you know that your relationship with your spouse deepens if you stay committed, you learn more about each other over the years than what you knew at the altar.

It's a similar scenario when following Jesus. Christians need to know why they are following Jesus. A new convert may not know much about the Bible or God and that is OK, they are drawn by the love of Christ. But to be a disciple, we commit to following Jesus and obeying His Word. Christians who still struggle with sin (besetting sin or unrepentant sin) have yet to count the cost in following Christ fully. The cost is our lives, our flesh, our sinful desires; we must give all of it up to allow the Holy Spirit to replace it with His will, His Spirit, and His desires.

With every decision we make there is an opportunity cost associated with it. The opportunity cost is what you are giving up making that decision. For example, if I cheat on my diet, I might add a couple pounds on for the next time I weigh in. Discernment in our lives requires us to know what we are giving up in order to pursue what we are saying yes to. Longer hours at work mean that we may not see our family as much. Neglecting the Bible consistently means that we are not as equipped to combat the attacks of the enemy.

God is not looking for someone who gets tricked into following Him. He wants disciples who count the cost and say yes to God despite what they have to give up in their flesh, because they realize their eternal reward and current peace cannot compare with what they might surrender now.

REFLECT: Have you fully counted the cost in following Jesus with everything in you? How do you need to "count the cost" in a decision that you are making or need to make?

*"Be very careful, then, how you live — not as unwise
but as wise, making the most of every opportunity,
because the days are evil. Therefore do not be foolish,
but understand what the Lord's will is."*
EPHESIANS 5:15-17 (NIV)

Have you ever had a tiny rock in your shoe? It is very annoying and even painful, but if you are like me, there are times you leave it in your shoe. Why do we do that? Well, it takes effort to remove the shoe and sometimes sock, find the pebble, when we can just "put up with it" even though it is uncomfortable. Logically, this makes no sense, just take 30 seconds, find the rock, and continue walking pain and stress free!

In the moment of an annoyance or frustration, it is sometimes easier to choose the lazy option instead of the option that will bring lasting peace. Lazy is easy. Paul tells the church at Ephesus to make the most of every opportunity. This means that at every opportunity we have for a decision we need to rely on God's discernment in our life to choose the best option. Like the pebble, why would we keep sin lingering around when we can just get rid of it, why do we hold the pebble so close when it is an annoyance and keeps us from walking in fullness?

We are not guaranteed a long life, in fact we are not guaranteed tomorrow. We have to make the most out of every day, every decision, and every chance at discernment because many times there are not second chances in major decisions we make.

Can we know the Lord's will? Well, the Bible says we can. This takes discernment as well as thorough reading of the Word and the revelation of the Holy Spirit. We know God's will for humanity, but we can also know His will specifically for our life. We have general revelation in the Bible as a foundation for our discernment, and the Holy Spirit can provide specific revelation to us as He sees fit.

Laziness will cause us to figure life out in our own effort and to cruise through it with sometimes reckless abandon. Laziness will also cause us to not care or not even try, going through routine day by day. As Christians, we do not want to waste the precious time we are given. We do not want to be at the end of our life and wish we had done things differently. We are accountable to the knowledge we are given.

REFLECT: What figurative pebble (annoyance or hindrance) do I need to remove from my life that I have been too lazy to remove? Why have I left it there apart from laziness? Pray about it and ask God for discernment on your next steps.

Day 13

> *"The way of fools seems right to them,*
> *but the wise listen to advice."*
> PROVERBS 12:15 (NIV)

I remember breaking up with my first real girlfriend or I should say my first girlfriend breaking up with me. I did not take it very well as I'm sure most teens don't. I felt some sort of personal challenge to prove to her that I was "the one." I'm sure I was overtly annoying even though I was subtly trying to continue to stay relevant to her life as a friend who still wanted to be more.

It wasn't until her dad took me out to lunch one day that I got the full picture. Here I am thinking that this lunch would be a way to prove my love for his daughter, when in reality he proved to me that I didn't know what in the world I was doing. He calmly shared wisdom with me in his dating life before marriage and how things worked out with his wife over time. He explained to me how it's important to leave things in God's timing and plan, and that if God wanted me to be with his daughter it would work out, but for now leave her alone (my summarizing).

I always respected the approach this godly man took with me where he had the right as a protective father to "run me off" from his daughter's life, this wise advice was the wakeup call I needed to keep things in perspective apart from my immediate plans.

God is patient and, in His omnipotence, He sees things from an eternal perspective, a way that we can never see things. God asks us to trust Him and believe even when we do not see.

Discernment comes from the wisdom of those around us who have a deep relationship with Jesus, who have been down the path we are going and can encourage us to continue or steer us to a better way. But it requires us to listen to this advice and take action.

Imagine the results of David lusting after Bathsheba if he asked the prophet Nathan for his advice ahead of time, obviously a no! Therein lies the reason why we often fail to seek advice, we are afraid of the ramifications it might have in our life and in our comfort zone. We would rather "figure it out" than rely on the wisdom of the people God has placed in our lives.

REFLECT: Who can you ask for advice and mentorship in your life? What is the reason you do not reach out to someone as often as you should? What specifically may you need to reach out for wisdom to someone today?

_____

_____

_____

_____

_____

Day 14

"And when people escape from the wickedness of the world by knowing our Lord and Savior Jesus Christ and then get tangled up and enslaved by sin again, they are worse off than before. It would have been better if they had never known the way to righteousness than to know it and then reject the command they were given to live a holy life."
2 PETER 2:20-21 (NLT)

Have you ever been imprisoned? I used to play cowboys growing up and had an amazing old western town literally in my backyard complete with a sheriff's office and jail. I remember when I would put shackles on my dad because he was the "outlaw" and put him in jail. One time in particular, I went into the house and my mom asked where Dad was. I had left him in jail (either knowingly or unknowingly I can't remember) and I had to go back out and release him from his temporary shackles.

Many in this life have physical and spiritual chains! Jesus has come to break chains, but if we purposely sign up for sin, we are putting the shackles on our spirit. The Bible even says we are worse off than before we knew the saving power of Christ! Why is this the case? I believe because we should know better. As Christians, we know the saving power of Christ but then if we reject a relationship with Him, we are to be pitied! This passage is not about salvation, it is about relationship!

Sin clouds our judgment and our discernment. If we are enslaved to something, it means we do not have the freedom to move away from it. Godly discernment requires that we cultivate a relationship with Jesus through prayer and getting to know His Word and the Holy Spirit. Can we be enslaved to things that we willingly sign up for? Absolutely!

As you move forward in discernment, ask what you are enslaved or imprisoned by. Often, we do not even realize what has a hold on us before it escalates. Are you slaves to sin and the flesh or slaves to Jesus Christ? What's amazing that when we are slaves to Jesus, we find our greatest freedom! This sounds completely backwards but if you've experienced it, you understand.

You might be in bondage to things from decisions you made years ago. Deeper bondage requires more strategic deliverance, but either way Jesus is still the answer. Even if you are a Christian, it does not mean that you are not in bondage. You may have a figurative tenant living in your spiritual house that you need to evict. An eviction notice requires a higher authority to deliver and enforce.

If you do not experience the freedom of Jesus, the love of Jesus, and the passion to pursue Him with everything you have, there's a good chance you are bound to something that is holding you back. Seek freedom today!

REFLECT: Write down some things from your past that you have been freed from? What might you be in bondage to now that you need freedom from? What sin in your life do you need to give an eviction notice to?

Day 15

"There is a way that appears to be right,
but in the end it leads to death."
PROVERBS 14:12 (NIV)

Have you ever been lost? Now in the days of smart phones and map apps, it's rarer than it used to be. People used to either have to know the areas really well or they would take a physical map with them (remember those?). We used to have the jokes about how a man never asks for directions until he is lost and then has to ask at a gas station for help at the prompting of his wife.

What's important to understand is that people don't start a trip saying, "I want us to get lost during this trip." Keep in mind getting lost is different than wandering aimlessly. I am talking about having a destination or a goal in mind, but you get lost along the way. I am confident the majority of Christians do not try to sabotage their lives; they simply get lost along the way.

Why do Christians get lost? They don't have the map, the Bible, as their foundation. The Bible is the roadmap allowing us to know when and where to turn, also Who to turn to! When we neglect the Bible, it is easy to get lost in our own efforts. What may "appear right" may end in death if we follow sin, our desires, or the cultural norms.

Now the Bible is not going to tell you exactly where to turn and what to decide. It will not tell you who to marry, where to live, or what job to have. The Bible is a foundation for our discernment. Discernment is Spirit-led decision making. If we neglect the knowledge of the Bible and try to follow our own plans (map), we will easily get lost from our goal of following Christ.

If you think about it, most people don't feel they are wrong, religions don't know they are wrong, people don't sell out to cults and false prophets because they know they are deceiving them. They appear right and there is usually a measure of truth in their false teaching. We have to be careful of counterfeits even in the "Christian Church." This is why knowing Jesus and the truth of the Bible are so crucial in ensuring we are traveling down the narrow path that leads to life.

If you feel lost and need help, don't let pride keep you from asking for directions!

REFLECT: What way in your past appeared right to you, but you found out it wasn't? Is the Bible your roadmap that you use daily? If not, what habits can you change to begin reading it daily?

"When you ask, you do not receive,
because you ask with wrong motives,
that you may spend what you get on your pleasures."
JAMES 4:3 (NIV)

If you are a parent, you know how kids can ask for just about anything and everything. They have no regard or understanding as to whether it is good for them or if it is within the family budget. They just ask, sometimes out of selfish motives, for things they want... I mean "need." Kids just need to have ice cream right before bed. Kids need the most expensive toy in the store. Kids need the vacation to a theme park and a cruise as well. Imagine if a parent said yes to every request of their child?

On the other hand, as a father myself, I love to hear the heart of my child. I love it when they ask for something I can give them, if it is within budget, will not spoil them, and that they will be excited about receiving it. I also love to surprise my kids with small items that I bring home that they didn't even ask for. I, of course, prefer when they ask and do not demand something, and also when they accept that no is no when the time is not right.

This correlation with our Heavenly Father to an earthly father is not a precise one to one comparison. God has unlimited resources and fully knows our hearts. He can see the past and future as easily as the present. We do know that He delights in giving good gifts to His children. God will also not give things that He knows will be wrong for us, even if it feels right to us and that we "need" it.

Jesus told the story of the persistent widow in Luke 18:1-8 to reinforce that we should pray and not stop praying. I remember how persistent I could be to my mom when there was a new toy I wanted. I had to "wear her down" so to speak when the initial answer was no. I had to convince her, who would then convince my dad, because if I went straight to my dad, it was a lot harder to wear him down.

How awesome that we have a God who hears our prayers and who knows what is best for us even when we may not on this side of eternity. We can trust God with our life and our decisions if we focus on Him and His purposes. God also loves it when we share our heart and our desires with Him. He wants to hear that our desires and will align with His.

Prayer should not be a laundry list of items that we want as if God is a cosmic vending machine. Prayer should be relational, committed, and earnest. We need to spend as much time listening in prayer as we do talking. If we believe in the power of prayer, our prayer life should show that we do.

REFLECT: Think of a recent prayer. Is what I am asking from God done with the right motives? Have I been persistent in prayer like I should be?

 **Day 17**

"Search me, God, and know my heart; test me and know my anxious thoughts. See if there is any offensive way in me, and lead me in the way everlasting."
PSALMS 139:23-24 (NIV)

Have you ever felt or said to God, "Just show me what to do, make it clear, and I will follow it 100%, but I need it to be so clear that I cannot mistake it"? I recently told God this about a major decision. My biggest fear is choosing incorrectly.

I even put out a "fleece" before God, asking Him to come through on a request to make clear a direction I should go. I would not recommend this as a guaranteed form of discernment. God has honored these requests before and sometimes He has not.

I thought about my kids and their chores. They are on a routine; they do certain chores on certain days every week. They don't have to ask me what to do when they already know what is expected of them. I get frustrated when they don't do what is expected of them or they forget. If they must constantly ask me what chore to do, and how to do them (when there is a schedule), I will just refer them back to the schedule. There are rewards for completing their tasks and punishments when they do not.

We can be like that with God, we want a divine sign, but many times God just wants us to be faithful with what we know we are supposed to be doing. Want to know what you should be doing? Read the Bible. Love your neighbor. Stay faithful to your spouse and honor your parents. Be consistent in your job and work as unto the Lord. Love the Lord your God with all your heart, mind, and strength. The list goes on…

Too often we want answers NOW, in fact we can be demanding. God is not slow to speak or slow to act. He does make His will known through the Holy Spirit and our growing in discernment; however, we often need to simply stay the course.

Many times, we just need to take the urgency out of the discernment process if we can. Major decisions should not be rushed; we need to exercise our discernment by reading the Word, praying, and seeking godly counsel. Sometimes God will give you a vision for something that is 10+ years down the road. Other times, it is to start something now!

There is no magic formula to conjure up an answer from God. It's about relationship, faithfulness, and patience.

REFLECT: Think about a major decision you have made or need to make. Write down the method you used to get to an answer, ask for feedback from an accountability partner.

_____

_____

_____

_____

_____

Day 18

"In their hearts humans plan their course,
but the Lord establishes their steps."
PROVERBS 16:9 (NIV)

There are two kinds of people in this world, risk takers and risk adverse. Which one are you? I am risk adverse. You won't find me skydiving or making a risky investment without carefully assessing the risk and usually erring on the side of caution.

As people we come up with all kinds of plans. We have big plans like who to marry, where to live, small plans like where to vacation, and how to invest your money. How many of a Christian's plans, both big and small, are prayed about and brought before the Lord? One percent? I'm not sure but I know that many often make their plans then ask God to bless them without ever consulting Him and asking for direction. I've been guilty too.

It's really sad when we blame God when our plans fail and yet never consult Him beforehand, how does God feel about this?

If you are a risk-taker, there are both positives and negatives that you need to be aware of when facing decisions and having godly discernment. The positives are: you are quick to move when God gives you vision, you see challenges as a reason to push forward and not retreat, you learn from failure, and are quickly ready to try again. The negatives with being a risk taker are: you may not wait for the right timing on a decision, challenges are not taken seriously with planning and forethought, and you may not listen to wise counsel that may persuade you against a decision.

If you are risk adverse, the positives are: you weigh risk vs. reward, you plan before you pursue which leads to specific steps of advancement, and you are less likely to fail and lose time and resources on a bad decision. The negatives are: you may lose a window of opportunity that the Lord is presenting to you by waiting too long, you stay in your comfort zone too long, and you persuade others to stay in their comfort zones as well.

The great news is if God is ordaining your steps and you are faithful and obedient, there is zero risk involved! I'm not talking about stress, setbacks, and frustrations, those will usually be present. The discernment process is how we get to the point of knowing God's will for us.

REFLECT: What did you learn about risk taking in decision making and how can you apply it to future decisions you need to make? What might God be asking you to take a risk on that you have been avoiding?

Day 19

"By day the Lord went ahead of them in a pillar of cloud to guide them on their way and by night in a pillar of fire to give them light, so that they could travel by day or night."
EXODUS 13:21 (NIV)

Do you ever imagine what it was like to be someone in the Bible? I wonder what I would have done in the same situation. I am often frustrated with decisions of those who sinned in the Bible, only to realize the sins in my life put me in no position to judge.

I look at the Israelites with frustration at how they would grumble, worship false gods, and wish to be put back into slavery in Egypt. I then realize that I have often wished for an old lifestyle and worship false gods by what consumes my time and desire. Stop it conviction!

The Israelites had discernment in their life through Moses hearing from God and through the pillar of fire and cloud on when to move. Often the Israelites would want to move from the place they were at, maybe they were tired of the location they were in and wanted to get going, but they had to wait for the pillar. Other times they wanted to stay put, they were comfortable, camp was set up, they were tired, but the pillar moved, and they needed to follow.

As Christians, we need to follow the move of God in our life. That means that we need to often stay put on an assignment God has given us even if we are bored with it and want to do something else. God is also great at challenging our comfort zones and moving us when needed.

If we stay put when God is calling us to move, we will miss the blessing that follows from being used as a servant of the Most High God. If we move without God in a new assignment that He is not in, we are in danger of failing from trying to be successful in our own effort.

We need discernment to know when to move and when to stay put, follow the voice of God, and keep His will above your own. A good sign in my life to move is when I've been in my comfort zone for too long. More than likely it means I haven't been pursuing God fully and would rather be comfortable than convicted.

REFLECT: Is God calling you to be faithful where you are at or do you feel a pull to move into a new season? Are you comfortable right now or is God trying to do a new thing in your life? Share this with someone who can stand in accountability and prayer with you.

Day 20

"As soon as Judas took the bread,
Satan entered into him. So Jesus told him,
'What you are about to do, do quickly.'"
JOHN 13:27 (NIV)

Have you ever made a decision that just seemed to come out of left field and resulted in overwhelmingly negative consequences? You may look back on that decision today and think, "Why was I so stupid?" With hindsight being 20/20, or so they say, it's easier to analyze your decisions after the fact, but growing in discernment will hopefully help us make the right decisions in the moment when it matters!

When you read that Satan entered Judas before his betrayal, it's easy to think that it was unfair to Judas, after all if Satan entered him what hope did he have in resisting?

The Bible gives us a glimpse of two ways in which Judas was already living in sin and not following his Master to whom he was called a disciple.

John points out that Judas was a thief, explaining that he was in charge of the disciples money and often took a little extra for himself (John 12:6).

Also, the woman who used an expensive bottle of perfume was scolded by Judas who said the money could be used for the poor. John sharply adds "not that he cared for the poor" (John 12:6). Jesus made it clear to everyone in front of Judas that the woman did the right thing to prepare Him for burial. Maybe it was Jesus' rebuke of Judas that led him into the hands of the high priests for 30 pieces of silver?

Judas had a haughty and greedy spirit, these open doors made it all the easier for Satan to enter him and hand over Jesus to the authorities. Yes, this was all a part of God's plan, but it is sad for Judas who was still capable of free will and let Satan control him.

We must be cautious to walk with Jesus and keep our eyes on Him. Seemingly "small" sins can lead to devastating decisions which can alter the course of your life forever. For example, take a man who deals with anger. One day he beats his wife leaving her in the hospital and him in jail. He may wonder in jail, "How did it get to this point?" The answer is by one small step at a time down the wrong path.

Don't give the enemy an open door in your life. We are ultimately responsible for our own actions whether they are influenced by evil spirits, strongholds, or just our own negative thoughts.

REFLECT: What do I need to take control of in my life now before it escalates out of control? Pray for an increase in discernment in everyday life.

Day 21

"Therefore, since we are receiving a kingdom that cannot be shaken, let us be thankful, and so worship God acceptably with reverence and awe, for our 'God is a consuming fire.'"
HEBREWS 12:28-29 (NIV)

Fire is amazing to watch. I have to admit; when I was younger, I was a bit of a pyro. I loved to set things on fire and see how they would react to the heat and flame. I never caused damage, but I can assure you that candles were quickly removed from the dinner table at my parent's house due to my experimentation.

Fire can be destructive; it can overtake a forest and cause massive damage. Fire can also bring healing, it can bring warmth, and it can cook food. Fire can be controlled to remove the debris on the ground of a forest which allows the vegetation to grow again. Fire can also be used strategically against fire, hence the term "fight fire with fire."

The Bible talks in many different places about how God is as a refiner's fire, testing us and burning away impurities. God used fire to judge Sodom and Gomorrah and God used fire to speak to Moses in a bush. The refining fire of the Holy Spirit can cleanse us of impurities, or it can consume us if we refuse to allow Him to move in our life.

We cannot easily discern the will of God if we are burdened with sin and the pollution of this world. We have to let God refine us. Many times, this refinement comes through trials. 1 Peter 1:7 discusses how these trials come to purify our faith like gold which is refined in the fire. No one likes trials, we want prosperity and blessings. However, the results of trials allow us to give glory and honor to Jesus in a way we may not have been able to before. The trick is to not become bitter when the trials hit.

If our goal is to give glory to God, it will result in us growing in decision making that puts us on a path of life instead of death. We can have discernment about our life if we keep our eyes fixed on Jesus either through trial or in peace.

Allow God to refine you, burn away the chaff that distracts and distorts the will of God. Cleanse your spirit with the Holy Spirit. Let God refine you in His fire now instead of resisting His cleansing touch.

REFLECT: How have I resisted the refining of God and what can I submit to Him today? Pray that God would refine you by fire in order to be able to bring Him glory with your life. Warning: do not pray this prayer unless you mean it!

Day 22

"God opposes the proud but shows favor to the humble."
JAMES 4:6 (NIV)

I'm thinking of a movie where there is an arrogant bully who makes life hard for the protagonist, but by the end of the movie, the hero puts the bully in his place, and they become friends united under a common goal. Which movie is this?

There could be hundreds of options you could think of to fit this time-tested formula for entertainment. We love to root for the underdog and to wish for the proud bully to be shown the error of their ways. Pride is seldom rewarded in cinema or in life for that matter. It may get you to a high place but often on the backs of many people along the way. Prideful people can only sustain this way of life for so long before the focus on self catches up to them and results in their downfall.

The Bible says that pride goes before destruction (Prov. 16:18). But why can't I be proud of my achievements and of the good things in life? The error in being prideful lies in the desire to bring ourselves glory instead of God. We need to remember that all things in life, including our gifts and abilities, come from God. It is acceptable to be confident in whom God made us, but it shouldn't cause us to make decisions without God in the equation. Paul said that he would boast about things that show his weakness because in his weakness, God gets the glory! (2 Cor. 11:30)

Pride and discernment do not mix; they are like oil and water. We might get away with pride for a while but know that destruction will come sooner or later. Often God has to bring the prideful to rock bottom so that they see that they are not equipped to handle this life without God, who gives us the breath in our lungs.

Not being prideful doesn't mean we should be depressed and timid to make decisions. We can have confidence in who we are in Christ and honor God with our decisions. God can use the humble heart to will and to act according to His purposes in this life.

REFLECT: In what area in my life have I been proud of my own accomplishments without giving God credit? What ways can I be confident yet not prideful? Confess, give honor to God and be humble before Him today.

Day 23

*"The prophet, along with my God, is the watchman over
Ephraim, yet snares await him on all his paths,
and hostility in the house of his God."*
HOSEA 9:8 (NIV)

Do you ever feel like you are trying to do the best you can,
but trouble just seems to find you? Maybe when you were
younger you were trying to be good, but a sibling would
accuse you of something you didn't do so they would look
good. Maybe at work you have integrity in all you do but
you have grievous accusations hurled against you because
someone is jealous of your position.

Many troubles in life we sign up for through our bad
decision making and even though they are still hard, we
tend to understand that we chose this path and are now
reaping the consequences.

What really hurts is when you feel like you are having
godly discernment and yet traps await you on every turn.
False accusations and temptations look to take us off our
righteous path. Just like the prophet in Hosea, snares await
him AND hostility in the house of God! It's understandable
when attacks come from obvious sources but what about
from people who should be serving God?

How often do Christians try to stay in the will of God and yet face persecution within the church? God may have impressed on you to take a step in faith and your biggest opposition (church and family) should have been your biggest fans. As hurtful as this can be, we also have to remember no one is perfect and the enemy likes to use people who we are familiar with and who we least expect.

Just remember that even Jesus was rejected in His hometown. Having discernment and choosing wisely does not guarantee an easy path. We know that following Jesus is the narrow path that few find. We have to persevere on the path even if it is hard because the blessings are often further down the road and some are not even in this life but in the life to come.

If you are facing snares from the enemy, understand that they may take human form, but often our battle is against spiritual forces. Stay prayed up, put on your spiritual armor, and do not turn back on the call God has placed on your life even if you feel like quitting. Discernment does not come strictly from our feelings. Perseverance is the will to continue despite your feelings.

REFLECT: What hardship am I facing in an area that I feel I am being faithful to God in? Am I staying connected to God during this time and listening to Him above all the other voices?

_____

_____

_____

_____

Day 24

"Therefore, I urge you, brothers and sisters, in view of God's mercy, to offer your bodies as a living sacrifice, holy and pleasing to God — this is your true and proper worship."
ROMANS 12:1 (NIV)

If you've played sports, you know there is encouragement that comes from coaches and players to get you ready for the game and keep you focused on the win. Some of the encouragement focuses along the line of giving 110% or not giving up. In order to win the game, you need to stay focused on the goal, stick to the strategy, and not be distracted.

Reasons for loss usually revolve around not doing these things. If you are intimidated by the opponent, abandoned the game plan, or held back physically, they are usually components of a loss. If you don't "give it your all" in a game, it is usually called out by the coach and if not fixed, will lead to a loss.

As Christians, we are called to give our bodies as a living sacrifice to God. The word sacrifice is not a pleasant word that we like to hear, and yet we are called to give our bodies (or all of us) to God. We cannot withhold a hand or foot, so to speak, and give God only the pieces we choose. We cannot give God pieces of our life and withhold our time, relationships, career, finances, desires, children, spouses, etc.

Indeed, God gave us His all when He gave us Jesus Christ to die on the cross for our sins. God requires it all from us; in fact, He deserves it all!

We are quick to sacrifice for earthly goals in our jobs, sports, for our children, for a spouse, and yet we are hesitant to fully sacrifice for what really matters, our eternal reward. Sacrificing to God is not about what you give up, but what you get when God is in control and the focus of your life!

God is not a cosmic killjoy. He honors our sacrifice and obedience with a deep relationship with Him that has a byproduct of clarity in making decisions that lead us to blessing right now in this life. It's not to say every decision will be easy, but as long as God goes before us, we know we are on the right path.

If we truly are offering our lives as a living sacrifice to God, we cannot protest when the knife comes down to cut out the flesh out of our life. The thing with a "living sacrifice" is that it can jump off the altar. God cannot purify us if we constantly get up off the altar and run away!

REFLECT: What am I still trying to withhold from God that I need to give over and sacrifice to Him? What are some reasons I hold on to control in my life without giving it over to God? Name some specific areas in your life that can be prayer points in sacrificing them to God.

_____

_____

_____

_____

Day 25

*"'Martha, Martha,' the Lord answered, 'you are worried
and upset about many things, but few things are needed —
or indeed only one. Mary has chosen what is better,
and it will not be taken away from her.'"*
LUKE 10:41-42 (NIV)

If you are married, the chances are high that one of you is
not at the same intensity level when it comes to chores. My
wife is pretty intense when it comes to keeping the house
clean with everyone on task and she does a great job at
it! However, I am more laid back, I find value in relaxing
and unwinding and do not have to be constantly on the go.
Many times, I have to convince my wife to slow down, come
watch a movie, or read that book she is working on.

I find in our Christian life we are so busy, and not just
with Christian things… the cares of this life and our busy
schedules seek to destroy our intimacy with God. This
scenario is depicted beautifully with Mary and Martha and
is one of my favorite Bible stories.

Here they had Jesus in their house and teaching them,
what a blessing that must have been! And yet, Martha
was so busy in doing things that she forgot to stop, relax,
and breathe. The Lord gently reminded her that she didn't
need to be worried and upset about so many things when
only one is needed, time with Jesus.

I think it's safe to say that Mary was not lazy, it's not that she would neglect her chores around the house at any other time. Mary knew when the time was to stop and rest, and that was when Jesus was present. In the presence of Jesus, we cannot think of anything else. We know the value of it as soon as we enter it, but too often we keep ourselves too busy to remember the importance of that quiet time. The world tells us we must go and do. Jesus tells us to rest and listen. The world gives us anxiety when Jesus gives us peace.

Even in the few minutes of quiet time we have with Jesus it's easy to be distracted! We start reading the Bible and get a phone notification, a kid starts screaming, or our mind wanders back to work! You are not alone in this.

If you are seeking discernment, find the quiet time where you sit at Jesus' feet. That intimacy cannot be bought or manufactured. It cannot be obtained by serving Jesus in a thousand tasks. It requires stopping and listening long enough for Jesus to guide you and speak to your spirit.

Once you have that intimacy with Jesus established, the tasks that are demanding your attention can then be done with clarity, diligence, and discernment.

REFLECT: When is my planned quiet time with Jesus and am I consistent in doing it? What hinders me from finding it consistently?

_____

_____

_____

Day 26

"The earth is the Lord's, and everything in it, the world, and all who live in it; for he founded it on the seas and established it on the waters."
PSALMS 24:1-2 (NIV)

Humans are possessive! Don't agree? Think about when someone stole your favorite parking spot, ate your lunch from the fridge at work, got the promotion you were working hard toward, or stole something out of your yard. But wait, I'm entitled to those things, so how is that wrong? Well, the Bible says we are entitled to death from our sin so we will not go down the road of entitlement...

This selfish behavior is not even trained, it is innate. If you have kids, you know how possessive they can get with a toy or a favorite stuffed animal when someone tries to take it. My daughter at two years old even yelled at my son for looking out "her window" in the car. I will admit that made me laugh though. My son told me one time at a young age to get out of "his room" to which I quickly reminded him who paid for the house.

It's natural to hold tight to what we have, not wanting to lose it. It is part of being a good steward to make wise decisions and not be reckless; however, the problem, as Christians, comes when we hold on so tight, with a closed fist, to what we have that we don't recognize that everything we have, even the breath in our lungs, comes from God.

We put limits on what God can have. God can't have more than this much of my money, God can't have my health, my job, my family, my kids, etc. God is not looking to take; He doesn't need anything that we give Him, and yet wants our heart.

We desire control. Control gives us a sense of peace and accomplishment. We say that our life is "out of control" when things don't go as planned. We set ourselves up for disappointment when life cannot match our expectations of it. Only God has perfect control.

Psalms 24 says the earth is the Lord's. Honoring God with our time, or gifts, or finances leads to a blessing and not in the way that the world may consider blessing. Only in the act of submission to God, when we lay everything down to Him, can we find the peace in knowing that we are not in control and God is.

REFLECT: What area of my life have I not submitted to God and told Him it is His? Do I have a thankful heart for what I do have and not envious of what I don't have?

Day 27

"For I am convinced that neither death nor life, neither angels nor demons, neither the present nor the future, nor any powers, neither height nor depth, nor anything else in all creation, will be able to separate us from the love of God that is in Christ Jesus our Lord."
ROMANS 8:38-39 (NIV)

How often have you heard the phrase "God loves you"? My guess is probably hundreds of times. Because that phrase is so commonplace, we often confine it to something said in kid's class at church or a cheerful slogan to put on a bumper sticker.

Do you believe you can never outgrow hearing that God loves you? Think about it; really think about what it means to have the Creator of the universe love YOU and want an intimate relationship with you. In fact, I challenge you now to take a few minutes to meditate on this topic alone. Be quiet and listen, absorb the fact that you are loved by God. Stop and do this now if you dare...

Are you back? Critics in Christianity will often challenge the phrase "God loves you" with Bible passages stating how we must repent and turn from our sins. We have to remember that in John 3:16, God so loved the world ... the world that was lost in sin and needed a Savior. It is true that God loves you as you are and also true that He loves you too much to keep you there.

When we focus on the love of Jesus and truly absorb the concept as much as our limited humanity will allow us, it should propel us to deepen our relationship with Him. We should be compelled to walk in obedience and to show that we love Him back.

Think of a married couple. The husband says he loves his wife on their wedding day. He says it often. 5 years later he's still saying it and showing his wife he loves her. At 20 years and 50 years he still says he loves her. Does the wife still love to hear it even after all those years? You bet!

Knowing our identity in Christ and our value as His creation made in His image, should cause us to think of our actions and decisions in light of eternity. We should desire to please our Heavenly Father and not grieve the Holy Spirit. We can't say we love Jesus back and then cheat on Him by our lifestyle. We don't have to make right decisions to earn His love, but our wisdom in having discernment should be a byproduct of the relationship we have built and are building with Him.

REFLECT: Do you believe that God loves you? How does this belief propel you to please God by your decisions? Write some examples in the Bible and in your personal life of how God loves you.

_____

_____

_____

_____

Day 28

*"For the Lord is the Spirit,
and wherever the Spirit of the Lord is, there is freedom."*
2 CORINTHIANS 3:17 (NIV)

Did you feel very free as a child in your parent's home? What about as a teenager? Regardless of the quality of earthly parents you had, children often feel limited and bound by the rules of the house that parents instill. An exuberant teenager might even say it is "a prison." If we had good parents, we find out later in life that the rules that were instilled were there for our own good. In fact, there's a high chance that we even implement many of the rules we rebelled against once we become parents ourselves!

Indeed, there is freedom for the child in their parent's house... if they come under the authority of the parents and obey!

As young Christians, we can often rebel against our spiritual authority, God, and think we know what is best. We think we know how the rules don't apply to us or that they are old-fashioned and not for today. Only a mature Christian knows that the freedom talked about in 2 Corinthians is "wherever the Spirit of the Lord is." The Spirit is everywhere but will not dwell in actions or thoughts that are contrary to the Word of God. The Spirit will not partake in activities or decisions that go against God's moral law. We are free to make them, but just like when you finally are free of your parent's house, you realize that you can literally make any decision you want. That is exhilarating... and also scary.

Sin easily entangles Christians who do not live in the freedom led by the Holy Spirit. We will never be perfect for only Jesus is perfect, but we strive to be like Him in all our ways and that includes our decisions.

What would Jesus do is not just a cool '90s slogan to put on a wrist band. We must be led by the Spirit in all truth and obey in order to live in the freedom spoken of in the Bible. To someone on the outside of relationship with Jesus it may look like bondage, until you realize those without Jesus are the ones in bondage to their fleshly desires.

So how do you get free from sin? I have found it is simple: sin stops when your desire for more of Jesus outweighs your desire to sin again. Too often we try to treat the problem without focusing on the solution.

REFLECT: Do I live in freedom by obeying the Word of God? Is there a part of my life that I have not submitted to Christ? Pray and turn that over to Him today!

*"Do not judge according to appearance,
but judge with righteous judgment."*
JOHN 7:24 (NKJV)

I think of the old saying, "Don't judge a book by its cover." But isn't it true that we often look through a bookstore and the cover is the thing that catches our eye? Remember when video rental stores were a thing? Looking at the front and back cover was the only way to get an idea for what the movie was about! You might see a cool action scene or a familiar actor and know that it was a safe bet to rent for movie night.

Jesus was facing judgment by the Pharisees for healing on the Sabbath; the Pharisees were judging based on the outward appearance of the act instead of seeing the heart of Who was standing in front of them.

Judge in the Greek used here is to "properly distinguish that is decide (mentally or judicially); by implication to try to condemn or punish." It is a natural reaction to judge others from a superficial standing. We make assumptions about someone based on their picture on social media. We see how others are acting at work or church and assume things without getting to know them. We react when our children are acting out emotionally without getting to the heart of why they are causing such an action. We argue with our spouse instead of realizing they had a bad day and just need time to unwind and relax.

When we walk in discernment, we don't react to these types of situations based on superficial appearances. We must look deeper at the heart of the matter. For example, that business deal that looks good on paper and everyone at work is telling you to do the deal? Maybe the Holy Spirit has different plans for you. Maybe your spouse needs to be heard on the matter. Maybe praying about the matter leaves you with a lack of peace even though the deal checks all the right boxes.

God looks at our heart and He gives us grace when we fail. We must be able to forgive and not react to appearances. Don't be in a rush to decide. Wait for peace and confirmation. Don't do what everyone does or says you should do.

REFLECT: When have I judged a person or situation based on appearances? When have I made a rushed decision that did not turn out well? How can I use time as an asset in making a better decision next time?

Day 30

"For the wisdom of this world is foolishness in God's sight."
1 CORINTHIANS 3:19 (NIV)

I think it is funny how many people, including myself, look back on their life and think how immature they were. If you look back 10 years ago, you might think, "Wow I had no idea what I was doing, I was foolish, etc." However, 10 years ago you might have thought the same thing 10 years before that! Not to mention that 10 years from now we will probably say the same thing about where we are at today...

No matter how much we mature, how much wisdom we gather, how much education we receive, and how successful according to the world we get, it is all foolishness to God. That's not to say God is not patient with us through the journey and celebrates our victories with us.

This verse doesn't mean to give up because nothing is worth the effort. The point of this verse is to understand that we need to rely on God and trust in Him. His ways are not our ways. As much as we think we know, we actually know very little. We are constantly learning and growing.

A.W. Tozer said, "Listen to no man who has not listened to God." The point of this quote I believe is to not let anyone keep you from the path God has put you on. You alone are accountable before God. When we try to have discernment about our decisions, we will have many voices that try to keep us off track and focus on human wisdom instead of God's truth.

There is a wonderful partnership with those who know God who can be a resource for discernment, but we must have selective listening (not the kind I use with my wife) when it comes to who is speaking to us and whether that voice differs with the direction God is calling us to walk.

Jesus called it a narrow path. Those who are on the wide highway will try to get others to join them; it makes them feel better about being on it to begin with. Stay focused for the reward from staying on the narrow path is life, both in this life and in eternity!

REFLECT: Is there a voice in your life right now that is not speaking godly wisdom to you? How can you minimize that voice or eliminate it completely? What is an example of "worldly foolishness" that you need to deflect with the Word of God?

_____

_____

_____

_____

_____

_____

_____

Day 31

"For the message of the cross is foolishness to those who are perishing, but to us who are being saved it is the power of God."
1 CORINTHIANS 1:18 (NIV)

Have you ever been faced with a decision that had two clear options (A and B) but you ended up picking a third option which was better than A or B? Imagine if a husband and wife were deciding on where to go for dinner. The wife wants Mexican food and the husband wants Italian. Neither one succumbs to the other's wishes. They end up finding a new Mexican restaurant that also serves Italian food! If only it were that easy, right?

Paul is writing to the church in Corinth and describes how the Jews were looking for miraculous signs to validate their faith and the Greeks were focused on obtaining wisdom. Paul points out that Christ is actually the perfect blend of both which is the "power and wisdom of God" (1 Cor. 1:24).

Christ became a stumbling block to the Jews and Gentiles who wanted Him to look a certain way to fit their needs. Christ can become a stumbling block in our life today when we want Him to meet our expectations instead of fully submitting to His will and living in obedience to Him regardless of the cost. For those that put demands on Christ that He won't or can't fill, they reject Him completely.

Discernment as well can be a blending of wisdom and revelation. Our human wisdom (attained through experience, knowledge of the Bible, and godly relationships) and power (insight from the Holy Spirit) when combined, can lead to powerful decision making. If we neglect one or the other, we are limiting ourselves in how we process decisions on a daily basis.

Some smaller decisions we only make with one source of discernment, but in the bigger decisions we need to not rely on our own strength. Trouble comes when we are too proud to ask for help and then we face the negative consequences of choosing poorly.

It's easy to rely on our own knowledge but it only gets you so far. We are limited by our education, experience, and overall humanity. There is freedom when you realize that no matter how much you learn in this life, it pales in comparison to the almighty God!

REFLECT: What am I trying to "figure out" on my own strength right now in my life that I need to turn over to God and rely on other sources of wisdom? How might I be limiting God in my decision-making process that needs to be expanded with the power of the Holy Spirit?

Day 32

"All Scripture is God-breathed and is useful for teaching,
rebuking, correcting and training in righteousness,
so that the servant of God may be thoroughly equipped
for every good work."
2 TIMOTHY 3:16-17 (NIV)

One of the most demanded tasks as a Father over the years seems to be building things. After Christmas, I must open and build the toys, I can't play with my ... gift card, I need to build a train table, build a crib, build furniture, and the list goes on.

Too often when I was undertaking a new thing to build, I would think, "I've got this." I would throw the directions aside and try to figure out the intrinsic details of the project by myself. I did this with my son's crib before he was born. What should have been an one-hour-or-so project turned to a 3+ hour project because not only did I ignore the directions, but I stripped a few screws by putting them in the wrong spot which led to a trip to Home Depot. After a time detour of not using the directions, I quickly grabbed them and backtracked my steps to see where I made the error.

Honestly, there's no reason not to use the manual except for pride and the belief that you know more than the company that made whatever it is you are building. You might get lucky on an easier project or something you have done before but a general rule of thumb is that you should follow the instructions.

The Bible is our "user manual" for life if you will. It contains wisdom and guidance that can be applied to every person living. Just reading the Bible does not lead to wisdom but applying truths in the Bible in obedience is what makes the difference.

We cannot be led by pride and ignore the Word of God in our lives. Too often people will head to the Bible as a last resort like I did with the crib instructions, however the wasted time in bad decisions cannot be recovered. God can and does redeem our past for His glory when we finally submit to Him, but it is wisdom to do it sooner than later and not waste any more time than we need to.

We only get one chance at this life. I don't want to waste any time, pay for any poor choices, or refuse to read and apply the Bible which our guide to discernment given to us by God... do you?

REFLECT: Do you have routines around reading the Bible for wisdom and applying it to your life? If not, what can you start doing today? When did you figuratively throw away the instructions on a decision you had to make and try to figure it out for yourself?

Day 33

"Therefore, from now on, we regard no one according to the flesh. Even though we have known Christ according to the flesh, yet now we know Him thus no longer. Therefore, if anyone is in Christ, he is a new creation; old things have passed away; behold, all things have become new."
2 CORINTHIANS 5:16-17 (NKJV)

Have you ever looked at a childhood picture of yourself and wondered, "Wow I don't look anything like that"? Or maybe you are more like me where I have looked remarkably similar throughout my entire life. When I was younger people would think that I was a decade or so older and now I can only hope people think I am a decade or so younger than I am!

For the most part, people don't change. I'm not talking physically, but their personality. It's shocking how close a good personality test can define you based on only a few dozen questions. Whether it's a personality test, an enneagram test, or any other of the trending leadership/ personality tests that rise and fall in popularity, we don't really change a whole lot as a person.

I minored in psychology in college and always found developmental psychology fascinating. The balance of nature vs. nurture in defining someone's tendencies and personality is a cause for much research and analysis. How do our circumstances and upbringing affect us in a positive or negative way? How does the personality a baby shows when they are only a month old define who they are for the rest of their life? And the most interesting part is the interplay between the two aspects of our development where the deeper study really takes place.

Even though I may improve in a category of my personality, I will always have tendencies that I have to fight, or I will give into them. Take being social for example, you may hate parties or large gatherings, but that doesn't mean you can't force yourself to enjoy a party (or at least fake it like you do).

How amazing is it that we are told that we are a new creation in Christ! The old is gone. The old sinful lifestyle, the old thoughts, and the old spirit. There is no other transformation that exists in the world that is as extreme as being in Christ! We will still keep our God-given personality and still have our history, but the difference is that we now need to lay it all at the foot of the cross as we focus on being more like Christ.

There are parts of this transformation process that are instantaneous and most of the parts take the rest of our lifetime as God works in us through the process of sanctification.

REFLECT: Do you genuinely believe that your identity is in Christ as a new creation? What does that mean to you? If we are a new creation, why do Christians continue to sin after they have found Christ?

Day 34

"He personally carried our sins in His body on the cross [willingly offering Himself on it, as on an altar of sacrifice], so that we might die to sin [becoming immune from the penalty and power of sin] and live for righteousness; for by His wounds you [who believe] have been healed."
1 PETER 2:24 (AMP)

I am frequently bombarded by comments online from atheists who relish in the fact that they sin and that they would rather "party" in hell than submit to God in heaven. Some even take the moral high ground above even God, claiming that God is not righteous or moral. Others will say that Jesus came to free us from sin, so they need to continue to sin so that He did not come for nothing. These types of comments only further prove the Gospel and human depravity that needs a Savior.

In Christ, we are a new creation, so why do so many Christians struggle against sin? Apathy is one of many reasons for this including misusing the grace of God. Taking the salvation issue out of the equation for a minute, it is definitely a freedom issue. Sin seems appealing and indeed it can be enjoyable... to our flesh. The quick pleasures of sin lead to a lifetime of bondage unless the cycle is broken.

Christ came so that we could live life and live it abundantly, not just in heaven when we die but here today! The weight of our sin is lifted off but just like weights in a gym, we have the free will to pick them up and lay them down. God forgives our sin and the eternal consequences of sin but that doesn't mean we can't choose the snare of guilt of our past and choosing to still sin that keeps us from freedom in Christ. The Holy Spirit gives us the strength and equips us to overcome sin, but it still comes down to our ability to keep our eyes fixed on Jesus.

In my book, *Everyday Discernment*, I have a whole chapter on discerning sin and the sin cycle. The sin cycle being that we sin, then we feel further away from God and so instead of turning to Him like we should, we turn right back to the sin and the cycle continues.

Satan is the king in guilt trips and so when we do mess up, we should come running to our Heavenly Father who is willing and ready to forgive. It's the same scenario when Adam and Eve tried to hide in the garden after they sinned. We can never hide from God so why do we try by ignoring Him?

God is the father in the parable of the prodigal son. The father did not wait for his son to get his act together and pay back his debt. No. He ran to meet him and threw a feast for him. His unconditional love for a son that did not deserve any grace by the wisdom of this world make his other son incredibly upset.

Not only does God show us love and grace when we miss the mark, but we need to do the same for those that God loves (aka everybody!).

REFLECT: When was a time when you were you caught in the sin cycle? What caused you to get out of it? What would you say to someone else that is currently struggling with sin?

Day 35

"This is what the Lord says: 'Stand at the crossroads and look; ask for the ancient paths, ask where the good way is, and walk in it, and you will find rest for your souls.' But you said, 'We will not walk in it.'"
JEREMIAH 6:16 (NIV)

There's a common belief that the current times we are living in are the best, that the people are the smartest, and that we are so much more advanced now than older generations. In some ways that is true as far as technology goes, but does technology equal wisdom?

I've been guilty too of reading books from long ago, even parts of the Bible, and thinking, ("Wow they were smart back then.") What a dismissive statement, as if anyone living before the 1900's was a proverbial caveman you see in cartoons. In fact, some of the greatest literature and works of art came from the Renaissance in the 16th and 17th centuries.

I've known some people who would not watch any movie that was made more than a decade before they were born. I always wondered why. There are some great movies made in the 1940s and '50s even though I don't seek them out on a regular basis. To be completely against anything of a certain period of time can limit our understanding of history.

This is also why "every" child when they become a teenager suddenly thinks their parent doesn't know anything instead of realizing that wisdom is learning from those who have more knowledge and life experience than you do. Not every parent is truly wise or a great source of godly discernment, but life experience cannot be dismissed either.

Studying war, for example, in history is fascinating to me. It's interesting to think of how a war could have been avoided if it were just stopped sooner. It has been said that if you want to avoid the mistakes of the past you have to learn from them and not repeat them.

Learning from the past helps apply wisdom to our decision making as Christians, to look for the ancient paths. To understand that God never changes, and His Word never changes. We cannot "progress" so much as a society that we negate the importance of these things. Discernment is, in fact, applied wisdom.

Don't look to society for answers to eternal matters, look to God and His Word. It's available for you today, in fact, more readily available than at any other time in history!

REFLECT: How might you dismiss the truths of God in the past as being irrelevant today? What can you do to find a mentor who can share wisdom with you about their life experience? If you already have one, what is one thing you have learned from them that is beyond your years of experience?

_____

_____

_____

Day 36

"'For I know the plans I have for you,' declares the
Lord, 'plans to prosper you and not to harm you, plans
to give you hope and a future.'"
JEREMIAH 29:11 (NIV)

The Bible is the infallible Word of God, but it also takes
discernment to know how to read it. It is a book of literature,
poetry, history, and prophecy. It was not written to us, but
it was written for us. I could do a whole series on misquoted
Bible verses with Jeremiah 29:11 leading the top of the pack.

It's important to remember that Jeremiah was writing to the
Israelites in captivity, promising that God will not forget
about them even though they have to go through hardship
in exile.

I've heard preachers say, "Just insert your name in a Bible
verse and claim it for your own." This is dangerous if
you do it at random without understanding the heart and
context of the verse. Good exegesis of the Bible means that
you need to know not just one verse, but the entirety of the
Bible and how the verses relate to each other. I've also had
people throw out random verses at me from Leviticus to try
and make an argument without understanding the place of
Leviticus in Old Testament law.

Now I will say that the Holy Spirt can quicken a Bible verse for you at a specific time and place and allow you to apply it to a certain situation. The difference being the Holy Spirit has to be involved as opposed to using a broad brush across the entire Bible. There's also general concepts that we can know about God from a verse that may have been Paul writing to a specific church but that we can apply today.

Even if we can't "claim" a certain verse for ourselves, we can find hope in understanding that we serve a God who does not change and is the same from everlasting to everlasting. The same God who had a plan and a purpose for the Israelites, has a plan for my life... but what is it? Is it prosperity? Is it a life as a martyr? There's a big difference between the two!

Stephen, in the book of Acts, had an amazing purpose, even though it led to death. His life provides an illustration for generations after him that a life fully devoted to Christ can lead to a peace that passes all understanding even during the toughest times of your life and the eternal reward promised to us is worth any trials we face on earth.

REFLECT: What is your favorite Bible verse? How could you apply it to your life while keeping it in the context of how it was written?

_____

_____

_____

_____

Day 37

*"Do not despise prophecies. Do not quench the Spirit.
Test all things; hold fast what is good. Abstain from
every form of evil."*
1 THESSALONIANS 5:21 (NKJV)

There is a critical spirit that has invaded the church that does not look like discernment and definitely does not look like the love of Christ.

What does this critical spirit look like? Let me give you a few examples. The church member that rushes to find the pastor after a sermon so he can point out where the pastor misspoke. The church gossip who is quick to point out that a new couple who is coming to the church is unmarried and living together. And the social media stalker who is quick to look up every post a church member makes so they can make a mental listing of all the things they post that they didn't agree with so that they have ammo for when the time comes to use it to their advantage. Do these examples sound extreme? They are not, in fact they may be more commonplace than you even realize.

The critical spirit is not of God, in fact it can be demonic. It seeks to destroy and not build up. It seeks to go on the offensive and not the defensive. It does not love. It does not ask before telling. It finds joy in winning an argument even at the expense of relationships.

Discernment is testing all things and holding to what is true. It is not a critical spirit, it is love mixed with truth, showing grace along the way. Often, discernment will not even announce victory at finding truth, but hide it in the heart that is only known to the Holy Spirit.

I have been guilty of having a critical spirit in the past as well. Frequently, my critical spirit would come in while I was listening to a sermon. I would wait with anticipation so that I could find something I believed was in error. I would then justify to myself, and even my friends, of why I was right. God delivered me from this years ago. I was only hurting myself. I never heard the heart behind the message, only what I wanted to hear.

I fully agree we should have discernment, in fact I have an entire chapter on discerning counterfeits in my book, *Everyday Discernment*. There is a time and a place for calling someone out in a sin or false teaching. The difference is that you need to make sure you have a seat at the table of someone you have a grievance with before bringing up a concern. If you are unsure what to do, lead with love and let the truth speak for itself.

REFLECT: How have you had a critical spirit either in the past or the present? What can you do today to have discernment without having a critical spirit?

_____

_____

_____

_____

Day 38

"This is the day that the Lord has made;
We will rejoice and be glad in it."
PSALMS 118:24 (NKJV)

My family and I would go to Disneyland every year. In fact, I never even went to Disneyland until I was in my twenties and then it became a routine. One of the obligatory rides I would go on for my kids was the Winnie the Pooh ride. Granted it is a cute ride, just not that exciting.

You might know one of the characters from Pooh named Eeyore. He is constantly in a negative mood and is a downer to everyone around him. One time, Eeyore responded to someone wishing him a good morning with, "If it is a good morning, which I doubt."

We have a lot of "Christian Eeyores" in the church. They are negative and would rather bring others down instead of finding the joy of the Lord and resting on God's promises. I'm not talking about having a bad day or clinical depression, but instead choosing a negative attitude for everything in life.

In fact, you can always find something to complain about. Take Disneyland again. If you focus on the amount of walking you do, the high (ridiculous) ticket prices, the waiting in lines, and the overpriced food, you will not have a good time.

When we view anything in the world with the optics of the world, it can seem helpless and hopeless. Our hope comes in Jesus Christ and that should bring us joy, no matter what pain we may face in this life.

Christians can choose their attitude when they wake up like the Psalmist and say, "Today is the day the Lord has made, and I will rejoice and be glad in it." When we take our eyes off Jesus and focus on the annoyances in life or the things we wish we could change, we lose our joy. It doesn't mean problems and annoyances go away and it also doesn't mean you can't try to improve things in your life.

We cannot have great discernment when we focus on the negatives in life without celebrating the gifts God gives us. Negative attitudes lead to poor discernment because we are basing our decisions on fear or self-pity. We also can't even see the move of God or want to be a part of it because of fear that we might fail or because it is new and out of our comfort zone.

Try waking up and thanking God before you get into the grind of the day, for His mercies are new every morning!

REFLECT: What would change in your life if you only focused on the positive and the blessings that God has given you? Write down what you are thankful for today.

Day 39

"But the Lord said to Samuel, "Do not consider his
appearance or his height, for I have rejected him. The Lord
does not look at the things people look at. People look at
the outward appearance, but the Lord looks at the heart."
1 SAMUEL 16:7 (NIV)

The concepts of movie stars and celebrities are still a newer term even though it seems like they have been around forever. With the onset of the silver cinema, regular people were elevated to a status level that no human has the right to be at. Hollywood was created and millions of kids and adults idolized these larger-than-life stars. This level of stardom often cannot be maintained without severe depression and other negative consequences.

Now, with social media, a teenager with little life experience who is handy with a camera, good with editing, and provides engaging content, can rise to levels of followers in the millions. This type of fame is unprecedented and is a dangerous example of making modern day idols out of regular humans.

What is interesting is that even in biblical times, people judged by outward appearances and God told Samuel that He looks at the heart. God is not impressed in the least by our number of followers, our charisma, our circle of friends, our good looks, or how much we can bench in the gym.

As Christians, we also should not be impressed by preachers on social media who live at celebrity status. It's not a guarantee that they don't speak truth (many times they don't), but that we should always have discernment in aligning what teachers of the Word say against the actual Word of God. Our awe with a certain person can put spiritual blinders on our eyes which makes it easy to take what they say as Gospel truth.

This is why when a falling out happens, and a celebrity pastor is in the news for fraud or a sexual sin, that so many people are devasted and even lose their faith. This is undeniably a sad situation when it occurs, and we should always be in prayer for the parties involved. The question becomes though, "Was their faith truly in Jesus or this pastor?"

We have to stay grounded in the Word of God and any external sources we get for encouragement and growth should be kept in their proper place, which is to strengthen our personal walk with Jesus. People can support our relationship with Jesus but they should never replace it!

REFLECT: Who do you make every effort to listen to what they have to say? Are you idolizing this person or are you truly using their words to strengthen your personal walk with Christ?

Day 40

"I want to know Christ — yes, to know the power of his resurrection and participation in his sufferings, becoming like him in his death, and so, somehow, attaining to the resurrection from the dead."
PHILIPPIANS 3:10-11 (NIV)

Have you ever read a biography or even an autobiography of someone? It might even be someone you thought you "knew" but once you read that book, it completely opened your eyes to all the little details of that person's life, their struggles, and reasons behind decisions that were made.

Abraham Lincoln is a good example of someone you read about in school and you get a general idea about who he was, but when you actually dig deeper into his life, you find that he was even more fascinating. He not only failed once but multiple times in life on his way to president and yet he never gave up. How much more could you learn about Mr. Lincoln if you actually got to sit down and talk with him?

Paul in Philippians is writing that he wants to know Christ. I always think, "If Paul did not know Christ then I certainly have a lot of learning to do!" Unfortunately, that is the familiarity we can think we have with God. We grow up in church, read our Bible, maybe even read a Bible commentary, and we think we know God. But pursuing a relationship with the God of the universe with our human brains means that we will never fully comprehend everything there is about God.

Now we do know enough about God through His Word to understand salvation and how to pursue a relationship with Him, but we never "arrive" and never get to the point where we can't continue to learn more in deepening that relationship.

I like the rest of this verse in Philippians because many read that we want to know the power of Jesus' resurrection and think "Yes, I want to see the power of God in my life!" and yet the very next part is to participate in His sufferings and be like Jesus in his death... ouch, well that part is not as exciting as moving in the power of God.

Some of pursuing a relationship with Jesus and knowing Him better is dying to our self, our flesh, daily. Only by doing that can we understand the holiness of God better and devote our lives to be used by God for His glory.

REFLECT: Do I have a desire to know Christ, to truly know Him more and more and not be content with where I am at? What is a sign that I may have become apathetic in parts of my Christian walk?

_____

_____

_____

_____

_____

"Then Daniel replied with discretion and discernment to Arioch, the captain of the king's bodyguard, who had gone forth to slay the wise men of Babylon."
DANIEL 2:14 (NASB)

Most days you don't have to go out looking for problems, they will come find you. Discernment is not only an offensive weapon but a defensive one. Decisions that we can plan out ahead of time give us the ability to pray, fast, and seek God and others for wisdom ahead of making the final decision. However, we are not always that fortunate to have time to plan.

Good leaders can think and speak on the fly because throughout the day many decisions require an instant solution without much discussion or thought. In the same way, most Christians don't plan to sin. Sin "just happens" which means we don't think about it and don't take time to let God guide us. We just give in to our flesh in the moment and we've all been in that situation.

It's important to point out that we will not get every decision correct that we have to make spontaneously. We will mess up and when we do, we should ask for forgiveness from those we hurt and also repent to God. I have found this especially true as a parent, I may be too firm with my kids because of how they are acting in the moment and I later have to reflect and ask for forgiveness.

In Daniel 2, Daniel was faced with a difficult decision, the king ordered all the wise men of Babylon to be executed for not being able to interpret his dream. The bodyguard came to kill Daniel and his friends, and the Bible says Daniel replied to this situation with "discretion and discernment." Daniel and his friends went home, prayed, and received a vision from God about the king's dream. If Daniel did not have discernment in this situation it would have meant death to both him and his friends.

The other important thing to note in this example is that Daniel praised God after he received the vision. How often do we forget to thank God when He provides wisdom and direction for us or answers our prayers?

The model Daniel gives us when faced with an extreme situation is one we can follow today for most decisions we will face: stop, pray, ask, thank. If we are able to take the urgency out of making a decision immediately, we can apply this process and proceed with wisdom.

REFLECT: How do you handle situations that require decisions immediately? Do you stop, if but for a minute, to pray and seek discernment? What things can you thank God for today?

"Now when Daniel learned that the decree had been published, he went home to his upstairs room where the windows opened toward Jerusalem. Three times a day he got down on his knees and prayed, giving thanks to his God, just as he had done before."
DANIEL 6:10 (NIV)

One of the most famous stories of the Bible we tell our children is probably Daniel in the lion's den. The imagery and wonder that fills our minds when we hear of such a supernatural story does such a good job at captivating our attention and filling us with faith in God.

A common response as to why Daniel was thrown into the lion's den is that he prayed when the law said that he couldn't. While that is accurate, it is but just a portion of the entire story. If you read at the beginning of Chapter 6, you see that the kingdom was divided into 120 provinces with an officer for each one. God had given Daniel great leadership and he proved himself more capable than all the others.

The other officers then went to King Darius and enticed him to make a law that forbid anyone to pray. It was envy and jealousy that led to Daniel being thrown into the lion's den. The king was tricked into making this law but also did not have the courage to reverse it when he knew it was wrong.

Daniel prayed both before and after the law was enacted. He would not change who his ultimate authority was, God, over a man-made rule. Remember, this is the same Daniel who is in exile and followed all the rules of the conquering kingdom... up to a point.

Following Jesus today will cause similar jealousy and envy on behalf of those who are not following Him and who hate the Holy Spirit that is inside you. The enemy works among these evil vices and will use sinful people to try to take you down through slander, persecution, or creating laws that make your faith illegal.

This persecution also takes place in the church under the guise of Christians looking to cause dissent.

We have to remember Christianity is in fact illegal in many parts of the world and Christians today are persecuted and killed daily for their faith. Remember Jesus said, "If the world hates you, remember that it hated me first" (John 15:18 NLT).

Having discernment will cause us to count the cost and follow Jesus no matter what the ramifications of that decision are.

REFLECT: Are you fully committed to follow Jesus in your life today regardless of the cost? Confess that to God today with specifics of what that will look like in your life.

_____

_____

_____

_____

Day 43

"Lord, I have heard of your fame; I stand in awe of your deeds, Lord. Repeat them in our day, in our time make them known; in wrath remember mercy."
HABAKKUK 3:2 (NIV)

There are many times in life when you hear about something and you try to prepare yourself, but the shock comes when you are actually experiencing it. For me it was college. I heard so much about college from my parents, the prep surrounding it, and yet nothing could really prepare me for day one. Walking around a mega campus as a freshman, I not only got lost, but I also marveled at the size of the campus and how small I felt in an experience that felt so new.

If you grew up in the Christian faith, there is a time for every child when the faith of their parents or pastor has to become their own. They have heard the stories of the Bible, the experiences of those who have shared their testimony, and it must become real to their own spirit. For some this happens at a young age as well and for others it may take years into their adult life for their faith to become fully realized. Sadly, there are some who abandon the faith altogether.

Habakkuk's plea is one I relate to, "Lord, I have heard of your fame." I know God moves and has moved in power,

has answered prayers, has changed the lives of so many…
and yet I say, "Do it again, Lord!"

There's nothing wrong to want God to move in power but
we also need to realize we have enough of a foundation in
the Bible to have all we need. We do not want to be like
the Pharisees that constantly wanted signs from Jesus. If
God never does anything miraculous again, we can have
confidence and faith in His Word.

And yet… there is a longing in knowing the power of God,
how He moves among His people for His plans and purposes.
Having discernment with what we believe means that we
often need to wrestle with our faith, to acknowledge doubts
when they come, and to lay them at the foot of the cross. It's
not a sin to doubt, however we do not want to stay there. We
do not want to let our doubt propel us into unbelief.

Let your doubts propel you to faith. Remember that the
God today is the God of yesterday and forever. Ask with
the faith of a child for God to do a new thing in your life
and move in power, not for a cosmic show, but for His glory
to be made known to those who do not yet know Him.

REFLECT: Is my faith my own or am I relying on someone
else? When did my faith become my own? Ask God for
something miraculous today!

Day 44

"But Samuel replied: 'What is more pleasing to the Lord: your burnt offerings and sacrifices or your obedience to his voice? Listen! Obedience is better than sacrifice, and submission is better than offering the fat of rams.'"
1 SAMUEL 15:22 (NLT)

Yoda famously said "there is no try" but honestly, as a parent, I love it when my kids try and even fail. Why? Because I know that is how a person learns. Trying and failing. Especially when I ask my kids to do something, I would rather they do it with a willing attitude even if they didn't get the results either of us were hoping for.

There's big difference when my kids fail at something because they did not try and when they fail at something that they gave their entire effort in. One is lazy and the other is just a part of the learning process.

In fact, when my kids obey a little too much, I have to wonder what their ulterior motive is, do they want a present, a reward, candy, or maybe they are covering their tracks before I find out something wrong they did?

One of the most frustrating questions when I tell my kids to do something is "Why?" It's not that they shouldn't understand some things, but there are plenty of times when I don't have the time to explain, nor do they have the maturity to understand. The reason "because I said so" is a terrible explanation but too often it is the easiest one to fall back on when children will not immediately obey authority.

You probably see where I am going here... God asks us to do things to test our hearts and to see if we will obey, even when we can't see the outcomes or know the reason why. Sure, God could spend time explaining every little thing to us but we neither have the maturity nor the mental capacity to understand the bigger picture like He does. Sometimes God will reveal pieces of His plan to us, but it is like looking into a foggy mirror.

God honors obedience. The results we expect when obeying God are often self-imposed. When God tells us to do something, we often extrapolate onto the results that will come. For example, God gives you a message to preach or a word to tell someone and we think, "This person will be saved!" or "hundreds will come to know Christ!" And yet... did God tell you what the results would be or did you tell yourself in your flesh?

If the only results that are achieved is that we did what God told us... then it is a success in God's eyes.

REFLECT: Are you driven by obedience to God or driven by results from serving God? What have you been disappointed in God for that was due to you placing your own expectations on a situation?

Day 45

"Which of the two did what his father wanted?"
"The First," they answered. Jesus said to them,
"Truly I tell you, the tax collectors and the prostitutes
are entering the kingdom of God ahead of you."
MATTHEW 21:31 (NIV)

Jesus told the parable of two sons. One that said he would not do what his father asked but did it anyway. The second son said he would do it but never did. As we discussed obedience yesterday, this is an important caveat in learning to obey and that is obeying at some point is better than not obeying at all.

Sure, Jonah is a terrible example of someone who ran from God and needed an extremely hard lesson in the belly of a great fish to finally get the message, but he eventually got where he needed to be. Discernment is so important because we can avoid the "whale part" of our life if we just obey God. That doesn't mean that we will never have trials or make bad choices, but at least we can avoid the hard lessons God needs to teach us if we obey right away.

We used to make our kids say when they were young, "I obey right away." Often this was said with an annoyed tone, but the point was that when they started arguing they would repeat this back to us to understand the importance of obeying authority right away.

The example we used is if they were playing outside and we yelled at them to run or get out of the street, it might be a matter of life and death that they obey right away if a car or a dog is coming at them! If they are in the middle of the street and they start to complain, ask why, or fall on the ground in rebellion, we all know what would happen.

Here's the good news though is that it is not too late to start obeying God right away. It may also not be too late to obey God in that one thing that you have been avoiding... you know the one...

The parable with the son who said he would obey his father and never did points out the hypocritical state of some Christians who mouth the right words, who say they love God, and yet live their life in rebellion to God and could not be bothered in commands such as loving their neighbor. I'm not talking about making a mistake and repenting, I'm talking about a willful state of rebellion to God's commands. Jesus even said, "If you love me, you will keep My commandments" John 14:15.

Let's all be the person who hears God's voice and joyfully obeys right away!

REFLECT: Think hard. What have you told God that you would do and yet never did it? If you can't think of something, what is something that you are not fully submitting to God in your life? Can you start today? Pray and ask for strength.

_____

_____

_____

*"It is because of him that you are in Christ Jesus, who
has become for us wisdom from God — that is, our
righteousness, holiness and redemption."*
1 CORINTHIANS 1:30 (NIV)

I only took one philosophy class in college, but I absolutely
hated it. It was nothing but seeking various forms of
knowledge without ever stating any conclusive statements.
Being a Christian, I already knew the truth, so the class seemed
pointless. This is what a lot of people do in their lives is seek
knowledge, they gather up knowledge like grain in a silo that
may or may not be used for anything practical other than trivia
games and telling others why what they believe is wrong.

The Gnostics were like this. Gnosis is a Greek noun meaning
"knowledge" or "awareness." The gathering of knowledge
in ancient cultures was often seen as the highest calling one
could have. Often, when someone gathers knowledge, it
does not develop into conclusive claims about what that
person believes. Many times what is left is all streams of
consciousness and beliefs lead to the same destination.

Many Christians are like this too, they listen to hundreds of
sermons over the course of their life and their symbolic silo
of Christian knowledge is full... and none of that figurative
grain is being used to feed anyone else or themselves. They

are spiritually malnourished even though they could access that knowledge and apply it at any time!

Thomas Watson said, "Knowledge is the eye that must direct the foot of obedience."

The knowledge we acquire from books, sermons, life, and even the Bible is only as helpful as our application of it. We must act in obedience in order to move from knowing into action. Knowing and reading the Bible is not enough because many well known atheists have an understanding of it but are not inspired by it.

There's nothing wrong with learning and growing in our knowledge of God, however, we have to understand that obedience to God should be our top priority even if it contradicts some of the "knowledge" we have built up in our own mind. God often makes the wisdom of the world look like foolishness.

In having discernment and making decisions, we have to use the knowledge we have gained and put it into practice. We have to be doers of the Word. Jesus is wisdom from God and when we are in Him, we have all that we need.

REFLECT: What knowledge have you found recently about God? What has God shown you recently through experience and/or through His Word? What will you do with this new knowledge?

_____

_____

_____

Day 47

"My people are destroyed from lack of knowledge.
Because you have rejected knowledge, I also reject you
as my priests; because you have ignored the law of your
God, I also will ignore your children."
HOSEA 4:6 (NIV)

President George Washington became severely ill in December of 1799. Doctors during that time believed diseases started in the blood and would eliminate "bad blood" from patients through a process called bloodletting. George Washington's doctors bled him four times in one day. A few hours later, he died. Today, most doctors know better than to resort to bloodletting.

This example makes me wonder how many deaths over the centuries were from the result of a lack of knowledge of medicine, technology, and more. Yesterday my point was that too much knowledge without action is foolishness. Today, my point is that not enough knowledge can lead us to make terrible decisions!

Think of a traffic stop. A police officer gives you a ticket for breaking a law you did not know about. Does your lack of knowledge get you out of a ticket? That is up to the officer but in general, not knowing the law does not mean exemption from the law.

Discernment is a spiritual muscle that must be trained and strengthened through the knowledge of the Bible, revelation of the Holy Spirit, and godly relationships that are speaking into our life. We also should learn from our mistakes and not make the same mistake twice.

Many poor decisions are made in life because the person didn't know any better. There's also plenty of examples where the person knew better and yet still wanted their own way! The Bible calls sin knowing what is right and not doing it (James 4:17).

The more we grow in our knowledge of God AND put that knowledge into practice, the more we will not only honor God, but we will cause less problems for ourselves by not making decisions that we have to sow the negative consequences from.

The Bible is living and active, what that means practically is that you are never done reading it. You are never done learning from the Bible. The Holy Spirit will highlight and illuminate verses for you and allow you to see things differently if you are listening.

As humans with finite wisdom serving an infinite God, we should never come to a point where we think we have nothing more to learn. We should always be teachable whether you have been in church for 50 years or 5 months.

REFLECT: What specific thing do you know more about in your walk with Christ now than you did in the past and how does that help you make better decisions today?

"As for God, his way is perfect: The Lord's word is flawless;
he shields all who take refuge in him. For who is God
besides the Lord? And who is the Rock except our God?"
PSALMS 18:30-31 (NIV)

I bought a lawnmower and not an inexpensive one either. It worked fine except the steering handles would constantly disengage themselves from the body of the lawnmower causing me to have to reattach them before being able to turn it. I was able to use the lawnmower, but I would have to reattach the handle quite a few times before I finished my small patch of grass. I was frustrated and I was in disbelief at the design of such a lawnmower. Why would this well-known company make such a frustrating product?

It wasn't until a couple years (yes, years) into owning this lawnmower that I saw a spot for a screw in the handle, tucked deep into the bottom. The added screw secures the handle to the base and eliminates the frustration I was having. It turns out there was a design that I was just not aware of. It wasn't the fault of the manufacturer, but it was my fault for not using it properly. In fact, I don't think I ever looked at the manual since it seemed pretty straightforward.

Once I realized I had been using it wrong for all this time, it made me think, "How many of us think that God is in the wrong when we really just don't understand His design?" Many people will put themselves in a blasphemous position of saying, "If I was God I would" and fill in the blank. Not only that but many throw out the "manual" to life which is the Bible either because they think it is irrelevant for today or that they can figure it out on their own.

Once you humble yourself and learn more about God through His Word, you start to understand that the things that may seem like a poor design is just because the Designer is misunderstood. We will never fully understand God and His ways, but we have enough information to know that, as the Psalmist stated, "His way is perfect."

We can make terrible decisions when we blame God for things or fail to realize the perfection in His design and that sin has come to rob us of joy and peace. There is a peace that comes when we can rest in the sovereignty of God and know that God has a perfect plan for us in eternity when there will be no more tears or suffering.

REFLECT: What is something you blamed God for only to later realize that He was not at fault? How can you trust God in the midst of a world tainted by sin? Make a foundational claim and prayer about your faith in God today!

Day 49

"But who can discern their own errors? Forgive my hidden faults. Keep your servant also from willful sins; may they not rule over me."
PSALMS 19:12 (NIV)

Have you ever listened to a sermon and thought, "Wow, I know the exact person that needs to hear this!" Or you might nudge your friend or spouse on a particular point that they need to pay attention to. I feel like it must be fairly common because I know I've done it.

We often fail to see the areas we are struggling in sin and focus on other people's sins. It's easier to point fingers outward than inward. It's also easy to justify why we are struggling by looking all the reasons that somehow make the sin OK.

This is exactly why Jesus said in Matthew 7:3, "Why do you look at the speck of sawdust in your brother's eye and pay no attention to the plank in your own eye?"

We often do things that we do not know are wrong because we have little to no awareness of how it is being received by someone else or how God sees it. This is why accountability and godly feedback is so crucial in our growth as Christians.

Good leaders will seek out 360-degree feedback, meaning they will ask for advice and input from those subordinate to them, their peers, and their supervisors.

The Holy Spirit is a better teacher than anyone. Don't suppress the conviction of the Holy Spirit. In our beginning verse, the Psalmist asked who can discern their own errors and then prayed for his hidden faults to be forgiven. We need to ask God daily for help in discerning our hidden sins and the things that we are so blinded to that we are letting them destroy us.

If you take a sin like anger, for example. The person struggling with it may know it is a problem, but not to the extent that others would attest to. They may not realize that anger has control of them and they may justify why they are angry to begin with. Here's a tip: If you justify any sin with "it's just..." it just needs to go!

Instead of deflecting, we need to reflect. Instead of being defensive, we need to be repentant. The next time you feel the conviction of the Holy Spirit in a sermon, teaching, or still small voice... listen!

REFLECT: Ask someone you trust to give you honest feedback on what you may be blinded to. Pray today for God to show you areas of sin that you are not aware of. Be still and listen to what God has to tell you.

_____

_____

_____

_____

Day 50

*"Do you listen in on God's council? Do you have
a monopoly on wisdom? What do you know that we do not
know? What insights do you have that we do not have?"*
JOB 15:8-9 (NIV)

When I was in my twenties, I did not have discernment as
much as I had a critical spirit. I could pick apart a pastor's
sermon and find all the "faults" with it. I could analyze
it while never really digesting anything for my benefit
or understanding the pastor's heart behind the message.
I analyzed it with a lens of my own perspective. Anything
in the sermon that did not mesh well with my biblical
worldview was either classified in the heresy pile or the
false teacher pile.

This sounds harsh and indeed it was. Keep in mind I did
not go to seminary or study much that would make me an
expert on any theological subject. I just weighed everything
based on my own limited interpretation.

Not only was a critical spirit present in my life but I played
around with sin. Not only did I easily condemn sermons,
but I failed to critique myself.

Job's friend Eliphaz in the beginning verse could not stand
the fact that Job disagreed with his friends who said that

Job's sufferings were because of a hidden sin in his life when in fact Job was blameless before God. Job's friends were not in a position to hear anything other than their own perspectives on God and suffering. In fact, they even mocked Job for his younger age than them, not realizing that age is not always an indicator of wisdom.

It's a tough balance in having discernment to have confidence in what you believe in but also have an open mind that you are still learning. It takes being humble and confident. Two terms that seem contradictory but in fact they are not.

We have to be open to the fact that there are always going to be things we do not know. God will move in ways we do not understand or have not seen before. God will give other's insight into things that we do not have. If it's biblical and of God, we should want it, even if it contradicts with our experience or education.

When you want to immediately condemn something, listen and pray before you dismiss it. It is also wisdom many times to not say anything at all.

REFLECT: When have you immediately dismissed a new concept or teaching about God without taking time to reflect on it and pray to see if it was accurate? How can you keep from having a critical spirit in your church?

_____

_____

_____

_____

Day 51

"We want each of you to show the same diligence to the very end, so that what you hope for may be fully realized. We do not want you to become lazy, but to imitate those who through faith and patience inherit what has been promised."
HEBREWS 6:12 (NIV)

I had a major career change decision in my life. I felt called to move in a new direction into full-time ministry, however I would be leaving my career field of 24 years. I had been feeling the call of God to move to full-time ministry for over two years, but I did not know what it would look like. An opportunity presented itself that kicked off a 6-month process of praying, fasting, and asking God for discernment.

This decision-making process made me realize that we cannot know with absolute clarity all possible outcomes, scenarios, and the future in clear sight. There is a measure of faith required when we move forward in what we feel God is asking us to do. Faith and discernment are NOT diametrically opposed to one another. Many times faith bridges the gap between what you know for certain and what you are believing God for.

Once I felt confident that I was moving in the direction God wanted me to, it did not mean that questions and fears went away completely. The beautiful thing in this example is that after I took a step of faith, there were numerous blessings that followed that I had not even factored into the equation.

God often gives us an open door to walk through. If we discern that it is from Him, it still requires a step of faith to enter the threshold. We can't see the next ten doors in our future, only the door in front of us.

There are times when an open door is not from God and through prayer, our discernment should register that it is just an opportunity but not a God-ordained one. There are also times when we need to make decisions that are just based on the common sense and wisdom God has given us.

Once you have a promise of God and once you know in your spirit where He is leading you, don't let the enemy talk you out of it. Take steps of faith and stay committed to that path even if it doesn't look like how you thought. Not all paths that God has us on lead to earthly prosperity and blessing, but that doesn't make them wrong paths.

REFLECT: What is a situation where you had an opportunity that you were not sure was from God? What was the result? What did you learn that you can apply to future opportunities and decisions you will have to make?

_____

_____

_____

_____

Day 52

"Have nothing to do with godless myths and old wives' tales; rather, train yourself to be godly. For physical training is of some value, but godliness has value for all things, holding promise for both the present life and the life to come."
1 TIMOTHY 4:8 (NIV)

I really enjoy getting a good workout. I've not always been consistent in working out, but I enjoy the feeling of getting stronger through exercise even if it is hard at times. After my son was born, I started getting in the best shape of my life. I was dedicating myself to intense workout programs that were usually 90 days long. I would complete a program, then repeat it or find another one to tackle. The feeling of accomplishment kept me consistent and energized.

My biggest struggle in exercise is not the moves or the commitment to completing the routine... it's food. My weakness is sugar. Soda, candy, and all their evil offspring. I can eliminate these for periods of time with intense self-control, but if left unrestrained, l will go right back to it.

Even though I had great results in my exercise programs, if I didn't follow the nutrition guidelines or if I ate food that was bad for me, including excessive sugar, my results would not be as noticeable as they could have been. Nutrition and exercise go hand in hand. Completing both the workouts and nutrition program with the same amounts of intensity allow them to complement each other for better results.

Paul tells Timothy that physical training is valuable but even more so is godliness. Godliness is being like Christ. It's being virtuous, righteous, and eliminating sin from your life. What we consume will impact our walk with Christ. If we live off spiritual "junk food" we will not get the sustenance we need to gain ground in our Christian race as disciples of Christ.

What is spiritual junk food? Things like social media Bible verses, quick prayers, limited fellowship with other Christians, lack of depth in relationships, or not committing much of your time in trying to hear from God.

Just as some junk food is OK in limited amounts, some of these things may be OK in limited amounts but we cannot live off junk food. We need the meat not the milk of the Word of God. We need to commit in time and energy to building our spiritual fitness just like we would with physical fitness.

Whatever you are passionate about in life, apply that passion to your spiritual walk and you will be on the right path!

REFLECT: List the things that you do in a month that might be considered spiritual junk food. What things on this list can you minimize or replace and what will you replace it with?

_____

_____

_____

_____

Day 53

"The Lord foils the plans of the nations; he thwarts the purposes of the peoples. But the plans of the Lord stand firm forever, the purposes of his heart through all generations."
PSALM 33:11 (NIV)

I worked in retail for many years and I frequently said in jest, "The only thing that stays consistent in retail is that it constantly changes." Often the plans I had for the day would be submissive to any figurative fires that would arise. These "fires" would take priority and I would have to quickly shift my plans around to make time for them.

It was still better to have a plan than to not have one at all. I knew leaders that rarely planned their days, and they would usually put out fires as their default mode. As a result, they would not get much done other than the fires that demanded their time. They managed at a frenetic pace without feeling a sense of control over what went on around them. They would also feel unprepared for future events that demanded planning and foresight.

As Christians, God has given us the wisdom and discernment to plan ahead in life while having a vision about our calling and the knowledge of the Bible as our foundation. Once God has set us on a path, we need to be good stewards of the call and move in the direction He is leading us. We cannot wait on God every step of the way if we know we are on the right path. God equips us with knowledge and giftings. We may also plan in our human wisdom based on our experience and education.

The important thing to remember is that God will often wreck our plans. We have to be willing to set our plans at the foot of the cross and pivot in a different direction if needed. If we are stubborn and try to force our will, it will most certainly end in failure and disappointment.

We have to remember that when God intervenes in our plans that it is normal, and we need to be ok with it. Only by being intimately connected with Him can this happen. Otherwise, we may take it as a personal attack on "our" plans.

God may also ask you to put aside a dream or goal you had in order to do something completely different. Will you be OK with whatever He asks of you?

REFLECT: What plans has God changed of yours in the past that required you to pivot? What are you planning right now to implement in the next year? Would you be OK if God asked you to give these plans over to Him?

Day 54

"Your word is a lamp for my feet, a light on my path,
I have taken an oath and confirmed it, that I will follow
your righteous laws."
PSALMS 119:105-106 (NIV)

As a kid I loved the *Choose Your Own Adventure* books! If you don't know what they are, they were books that you would not read chronologically, page by page. You would get to a part of the story and it would leave you with options like turn left or right, climb the mountain or go through the swamp, fight the bear or hide in the bear cave. There were numerous books in the series and most of them involved danger at some level.

Once you made a decision in the book, it would have you skip to a specific page number which would continue the story just to face more options. At some point in the story the reader usually died or lost their way and they had to backtrack to the previous decision in order to try and finish the story with a happy ending.

These books provided a sense of immersion that was not offered in video games at the time. I loved video games too, but they were limiting on decision making to usually just Move and Fire. Seeing the impact of my decisions play out in a book was exciting at the time even though there are much more immersive story experiences now.

Enter adulthood. Every day is immersed in decisions, albeit not as fun as fighting off a pack of monkeys or scaling a volcano... The important thing I remember about the adventure books is that your previous decision didn't really help you in your current one. You couldn't rely on what you did in the past for your current situation.

How much more so in our Christian faith do we need daily wisdom on decisions we make? Our victories or failures in the past may have put us on the path we are on, but we still have to make the right decision each and every day. This can be tiring!

Think of yourself in a dark corridor in an adventure book, your only source of light is the Word of God. This is the picture I get from the Psalmist in our beginning verse today. Following God's laws keeps us on the right path for us. Each decision we make is important (some more than others). We can't cruise along based on what we did in the past and we cannot let our guard down.

REFLECT: What are some examples of bigger decisions that you make weekly? Are those decisions made with prayer and reflection on the Word of God or just in your own effort? What decision is coming up that you can give over to God right now in prayer?

Day 55

"Brothers and sisters, I do not consider myself yet to have taken hold of it. But one thing I do: Forgetting what is behind and straining toward what is ahead, I press on toward the goal to win the prize for which God has called me heavenward in Christ Jesus."
PHILIPPIANS 3:13-14 (NIV)

It's an understatement to say that cars have advanced since I started driving. They now have advanced computers and sensors to the point where some cars even can drive themselves. I never had a computerized maintenance schedule that would remind me when it was time for a tire rotation or an oil change. I would use an old checking balance book in my glove compartment and write down all the maintenance that was accomplished and on what mileage. I didn't even have a smart phone that I could enter a note or a reminder into.

Now cars have sensors that tell you when maintenance is needed, tire pressure is too low, and the all too familiar check engine light which sometimes comes on just because it likes to be annoying. If you know your car, you can also listen for strange sounds or the way the car controls to get an idea that something is off.

Not paying attention to these warning signs on your car for too long can lead to getting stranded or costly bills. Getting maintenance done proactively or when there is a sign of a warning can save you money and time in the long run.

There are often figurative warning lights that go off in our life that we need to listen to. Many times, this is the Holy Spirit quickening things to us that we need to stop and take care of before we press onward.

Conviction is often a work of the Holy Spirit. Things that previously we did without conviction that now leave us feeling guilty can be a God sign that we need to abandon them and keep our eyes on Jesus.

In having discernment and making better decisions, we must listen to the conviction of God in our lives. To do this, we need to stay close to God daily. We need to be quiet and not surrounded by so many distractions that we quickly ignore the warning signs. Convictions are between you and God. What everyone else is doing does not matter when it comes to being faithful and obedient to what God is calling you to do.

Not dealing with sin in a timely manner can leave you with costly mistakes that could have been prevented. It's not enough to justify sin with the fact that you used to do it without worry. If you now have conviction about something, don't dismiss it, repent.

REFLECT: What Holy Spirit warnings have you listened to regarding something you were doing and what did you change because of it? What have you been feeling convicted about lately that you might need to pray about getting an action plan together to change?

Day 56

*"Do not store up for yourselves treasures on earth,
where moths and vermin destroy, and where thieves
break in and steal. But store up for yourselves treasures
in heaven, where moths and vermin do not destroy, and
where thieves do not break in and steal. For where your
treasure is, there your heart will be also."*
MATTHEW 6:19-21 (NIV)

I casually follow the stock market, not really for any purpose other than a hobby. I find following businesses interesting and learning what makes the stock market fluctuate on a daily basis, some of it is strategic, yet most of it is a gamble.

I came across an interesting concept relating to stocks. All stocks fluctuate up or down, even stocks that consistently go up over time. Take Google for example, which started somewhere around $30 and is now over $2000 at the time of this writing, the path upwards is not a straight line, there is something called "resistance". If a stock is going through resistance, it goes up for a bit and then comes down, this allows investors who are trading to take any profit out of the jump in price and sell their shares to either buy again later or abandon the stock completely. The concept of resistance is when a stock falls after hitting a ceiling and a support level is when a stock falls to the point of investors wanting to buy back in.

Stocks along with any type of finances or wealth are all temporary as the verse above describes. What really matters is our eternal, heavenly investment in Jesus. When we accept Him as our Savior, we establish our names in the book of Life. As a Christian, we too, face "resistance". It is not just a straight shot to heaven without any pain or worries. If we believe we have "invested" in the right future with Jesus, we will hold fast to Him and not be shaken when we hit resistance.

Christians that face trials and tribulations will be tempted to "sell" and "cut their losses" and end up losing out on our glorious reward. Remember the support level of stocks that once they drop, investors will start buying again. If we hit resistance and hold fast, we will hit the "support" level where Jesus will see us through our struggles if we hold onto Him.

Have you made the right investment? If you've invested in Jesus, don't give up when you hit resistance. Stay steadfast, keep your eyes on Jesus, and you will receive your reward!

Our reward as Christians is not just an eternity with our Savior but a life with Him now, living in freedom from bondage and finding joy in serving others in love.

REFLECT: What are some examples in your life when you hit resistance? What are some examples where you had support from either God or fellow Christians to get you through struggles?

_____

_____

_____

_____

*"The Lord rewards everyone for their righteousness
and faithfulness. The Lord delivered you into my
hands today, but I would not lay a hand on the Lord's
anointed. As surely as I valued your life today, so may
the Lord value my life and deliver me from all trouble."*
1 SAMUEL 26:23-24 (NIV)

God had enough of Saul and his disobedience saying, "I regret that I have made Saul king, because he has turned away from me and has not carried out my instructions" (1 Samuel 15:11). Samuel anointed David even before he became king, David then defeated Goliath and the jealousy of Saul began to form. Saul tried to kill David multiple times and had him on the run. David was given the opportunity to kill Saul. Here David had been given the choice to end his fleeing, to speed God's plan for him to be king, to take vengeance against a man whom God's anointing had already left. David did not use this opportunity as an excuse to sin, he took the high ground. David even had a second chance to kill Saul in Chapter 26 and his own men even cheered him on to kill Saul.

David's action, or inaction, resulted in a mending (albeit brief) of his relationship with Saul. Saul apologized and said to David, "May you be blessed, David my son; you will do great things and surely triumph" (1 Samuel 26:25). Now the story of Saul did not end happily, he consulted a medium in

Chapter 28 and died of suicide on the battlefield in Chapter 30, but it wasn't at the hand of David. David saw ahead at the tragic plan for Saul, but he wasn't going to sin to be a part of it, it wasn't something that God was commanding him to do, and David wasn't going to rush God's timeline. David had his convictions and would not try and hurry up something God didn't need his help with. The opportunity of being able to kill Saul two times might have been too much for most people to ignore, but not David.

We need to view the act of having an opportunity to do something not as validation for doing it. We need to view the opportunity in light of the Bible, in light of God's calling on our lives, and in light of God's direction. Major opportunities decided in haste will often lead to negative consequences. We might be presented with a new job that is not right for our family, a chance at vengeance over someone that hurt us, an opportunity to give into lust without being caught, or to give into anger and hurt those around us. Do not confuse being given an opportunity as a divine appointment being handed to you. When in doubt pray and use the Bible as a filter for every decision.

REFLECT: Do I rush into my decisions daily or do I pray about them? Do I consider having the opportunity to do something as an excuse to sin? How can I change how I view opportunity in the future?

_____

_____

_____

_____

Day 58

*"Enter through the narrow gate. For wide is the gate
and broad is the road that leads to destruction, and many
enter through it. But small is the gate and narrow the
road that leads to life, and only a few find it."*
MATTHEW 7:13-14 (NIV)

I frequently hear from one of my kids that something is "not
fair" or "too hard", I'm sure most parents who hear this roll
their figurative or literal eyes at this while they think, "if you
only knew!" To children, they don't seem to understand that
just because something is hard, does not mean that you give
up. As a parent, you should take the opportunity to train
them on this with the hope that by the time they face real,
hard challenges in life, they will persevere through them.

In 2 Kings 5, Naaman was the leader of the Syrian army, but he
had leprosy. A captive Israelite girl, who knew of the prophet
Elisha and his miracles, told Naaman to send for Elisha to be
cured of his leprosy. Naaman sent a letter to the King of Israel
to announce his arrival and to ask for healing, Elisha heard
of this and invited Naaman to come to his house. Elisha's
servant met Naaman at the door and instructed Naaman to,
"Go, wash yourself seven times in the Jordan, and your flesh
will be restored, and you will be cleansed" (v.10).

Here Elisha gave Naaman a cure for the disease that plagued
him. Naaman went away angry and said, "I thought that he
would surely come out to me and stand and call on the name

of the Lord his God, wave his hand over the spot and cure me of my leprosy. Are not Abana and Pharpar, the rivers of Damascus better than all the waters in Israel? Couldn't I wash in them and be cleansed?" (v.11-12)

Luckily for Naaman, his servants talked some sense into him and said, "My father, if the prophet had told you to do some great thing, would you not have done it? How much more, then, when he tells you, 'Wash and be cleansed'!" (v.13). Naaman went and did what was instructed and his skin became like that of a "young boy." Naaman said, "Now I know that there is no God in all the world except in Israel" (v.15).

Naaman in this story is an example of how obedience is important even if we do not understand why. If we trust in Who we don't need to know why. Naaman wanted a figurative snap of Elisha's fingers to fix his problems. He didn't want to wash seven times in a river that was a considerable distance away from where he was. To Naaman the logical solution seemed to be the easiest and quickest one, but God's glory would be revealed through his obedience to the prophet.

How often do we pray today and expect an easy answer to a problem? How many people today read the Bible and say, "That's too hard!" God expects obedience and sometimes He tests us to see if we are faithful.

REFLECT: What has God told me to do before that seemed drastic, but it worked out after I was obedient? What am I asking for today that I need to seek God's will on? Commit to obeying God even if it seems hard.

$$\mathcal{D}ay \; 59$$

*"Listen to advice and accept discipline, and at the end you
will be counted among the wise. Many are the plans in
a person's heart, but it is the Lord's purpose that prevails."*
PROVERBS 19:20-21 (NIV)

My newest car has an amazing feature that makes me
wonder what I did without it before. On the side mirrors,
there is a light that illuminates when a car is in the blind
spot on either the right or the left side. Such a simple design
and yet it potentially can save many lives from accidents
including saving your neck from having to turn and double
check. It even gives a warning beep if you put on your turn
signal and there is a vehicle in your blind spot.

Blind spots are only hidden to the driver of the car.
Everyone else around and behind the car can see the cars
but it doesn't matter because they can't warn the driver of
the potential danger.

We all have blind spots in our lives. Hidden areas that we
are oblivious to or that we just don't want to take the time to
check on and deal with. These hidden areas, if not checked,
can lead to disaster and heartache. Things like hidden
anger, lust, trauma, resentment, bitterness, unforgiveness,
and much more can hide in wait until it's time to derail
your movement.

Great leaders will seek to expose their blind spots before their blind spots expose them! They will ask for input from their subordinates, their peers, and their supervisors. This will help root out any blind spots in their leadership that one group of people may not see or may not feel comfortable sharing.

It's similar to speech class in school when you gave a speech and thought you did awesome and then you were forced to watch it. Upon viewing the speech, you were able to see all the problems with it which you then could work on improving for the next time. Also the teacher who taught speech class for years, would have even more insight based on his or her experience and seeing hundreds of other presentations.

Godly counsel in our lives can speak wisdom into the blind spots of our lives and many times it is up to us to ask for it. It may not be fun to hear but if it is said with love, you can create an action plan to eliminate these blind spots before you take an action that you will regret.

REFLECT: What blind spots are you aware of or have you dealt with in the past? Who can you ask to help give you regular feedback on your Christian walk in order to root out blind spots before they get to be a problem?

 Day 60

"If any of you lacks wisdom, you should ask God, who gives generously to all without finding fault, and it will be given to you. But when you ask, you must believe and not doubt, because the one who doubts is like a wave of the sea, blown and tossed by the wind."
JAMES 1:5-6 (NIV)

Did you ever notice how grocery stores are laid out? There's a reason the milk is on the other side of the store from the bread. The store designers want you to walk through as much of the store as possible so that you can be seduced by impulse purchases.

This is one of the reasons my wife doesn't send me shopping too often. I may go in for 10 things and come out with 20 because I love to try new items or new variations on brands I like. A new flavor Oreo or M&Ms is usually a must buy.

The checkout lanes also are well designed for impulse purchases. The candy and random toy are usually at the eye sight of a younger child who can then start to plead with their parents to buy it while the parent is busy trying to check out. I worked in retail for many years, and I saw the power of these last-minute sections as they often led to screaming children after a parent said no.

The power of these last-minute sections is that children would ask. I've never seen a parent volunteer to feed their kid chocolate and sugar that wasn't on the shopping list without the child asking.

Did you ever think that a part of having discernment is just asking? I often say that discernment is a spiritual muscle that must be trained, and while that is true, James makes it clear that, "If any of you lacks wisdom, you should ask God."

Solomon is the greatest example of this. He was a king that could have asked God for anything and he asked for wisdom. Through that wisdom he was able to lead his kingdom to tremendous success.

Stopping and praying for wisdom in our daily life is not a one-time event though. We have to be tuned into the will of God and be led by the Holy Spirit.

Before facing a decision, pray and ask God for wisdom. Before you enter that meeting at work, ask God for wisdom. Before you go reprimand your kids for causing problems downstairs, ask God for wisdom. Before you try to repair a relationship, stop, and ask God for wisdom. Before you write a reply to that rude email or comment on that post on social media, stop and ask God for wisdom.

REFLECT: How often do you stop and ask God for wisdom in your day? What key times in your schedule would be a good time to take a minute and pray for wisdom? Take time now to pray for wisdom before you continue your day.

_____

_____

_____

*"Because we have these promises, dear friends, let
us cleanse ourselves from everything that can defile
our body or spirit. And let us work toward complete
holiness because we fear God."*
2 CORINTHIANS 7:1 (NLT)

I don't hate going to the dentist's office, but it's definitely not enjoyable. Sure, my teeth feel great after and I get a free toothbrush, but they always tell me the stuff I'm not doing that I should be doing. Brush twice a day, floss every day, limit the sugary food and drink. I just simply smile and say, "I'll do better."

I kept ignoring the dentist's warnings because, well, it's too much work. Sure, they had good points and much more education on teeth than I have but I chalk it up to the, "I'll deal with it later" mentality. On one visit I had 5 cavities and I instantly regretted not taking the extra steps to prevent my teeth from getting to this point. I also had my first crown which was not fun. Since then, I floss every day and even got an electric water pick upon their suggestion. Unfortunately, a lot of the damage was already irreparable.

The Bible tells us to cleanse ourselves of things that can defile our body or spirit. This takes a lot of work and devotion. We might be tempted to push the standard back and do it when we have more time or after we enjoy what this world has to offer. The problem comes when we have to pay for that with the consequences of the mistakes we make and the wasted time when we could be pursuing God.

It's easy to read something in the Bible or to hear a sermon and think that the message doesn't apply to you. It's the Holy Spirit's job to convict and our job to listen and act.

It takes work to be holy. Holiness does not just happen. Receiving salvation does not sanctify you, it is a process. The Bible outlines many ways we can be holy before an almighty God. We have to trust God at His Word and follow the guidelines He gives us to live our life to the fullest in Him!

We must fight the urge to dismiss wisdom and call it foolishness. Things in life worth doing are worth doing well and the same thing goes for a life dedicated to Jesus. Nothing else in this world will bring the fulfillment to our soul.

If Jesus is not enough, nothing else in this world ever will be!

REFLECT: What instructions of the Bible have you been ignoring even though you know they are good for you? What steps can you make today to start following them?

_____

_____

_____

_____

_____

Day 62

*"So humble yourselves under the mighty power of God,
and at the right time he will lift you up in honor. Give all
your worries and cares to God, for he cares about you."*
1 PETER 5:6-7 (NLT)

With my personality and temperament, I like to internalize a lot of what I am thinking. Usually this occurs to the point where I have so much on my mind that it creates a lot of stress. It piles up like files to be processed on a desk spilling over at the sides.

My wife usually picks up on this and asks me what is on my mind. I justify to myself that I don't want to bother her, so I don't usually let it out on the first time she asks. She then will sit me down and inquire, "What are three things that are worrying you right now?" At this point I give in and spit it out. Instantly I feel better for giving these problems a voice and for having someone on the other end listening to me.

In 1 Peter, the Bible says to give your worries to God or cast your cares to God because He cares for you. Psalm 55:22 says a similar thing, "Give your burdens to the Lord, and he will take care of you. He will not permit the godly to slip and fall."

Everyone has burdens and worries; some days are worse than others. There may be relationship problems, financial burdens, an unsaved loved one, health problems, major decisions at work, and many more. The idea of giving or casting your worries to God is an action. It is a verb. It requires something of us in order to give them to God... we have to let them go.

God will not come and pry our worries out of our hands against our will. We are commanded to give them to Him, to set them at the foot of the cross. God cares about you. Don't believe the lie that your burdens are insignificant or that God does not care about intimate details of your life. Rebuke those lies verbally. There is power in our words when we speak. When you have burdens, speak them out to God, let the enemy hear you release them.

The trick then becomes to not pick up the burden again once you set it at the cross. Giving burdens to God does not mean that we take no action on the situation but that we listen to the voice of God for discernment. We acknowledge the fact that we don't have the answers and that we can't figure it out on our own. We need our Savior's help.

REFLECT: What burdens do you have now that you can verbally release to God? Ask for prayer in confirmation and agreement with someone else once you release it.

_____

_____

_____

_____

_____

_____

Day 63

"My ears had heard of you but now my eyes have seen you."
JOB 42:5 (NIV)

I've met a few celebrities in my life and what people always ask me is, "What were they like?" Keep in mind these are celebrities that anyone can read the life story of online and know the details of their career, childhood, interviews, and more. What people are really asking when you meet someone famous is if the person lives up to their reputation. Were they rude, nice, friendly, did they take a picture with you, did they sign an autograph? Even meeting someone for a few minutes does not constitute truly knowing someone, but it gives you a better perspective on who they are compared with what you have seen or heard on TV or read about on the Internet.

At the end of Job, Job has gone through this huge ordeal of tragedy, pain and suffering, and friends who gave him horrible advice. Finally, God reveals Himself in a whirlwind with many questions to Job that solidify the fact that Job knows nothing of the ways of God. God never answers all of Job's questions, but affirms the fact that Job has no right to question God's ways.

What I find fascinating is that here Job was, the most righteous person on the planet, which is why Satan asked to tempt him with pain. At the end of the book, Job confesses that he had only heard of God but finally had seen Him.

Job was using the difference between hearing and seeing to compare his comprehension level with Who God actually is! Hearing about someone is different than experiencing them face to face. As righteous as Job was, he didn't know God with the understanding he eventually had until after his terrible ordeal.

Just as someone can read all about the details of a celebrity without actually knowing them as a person, someone can read all about God in the Bible without ever experiencing Him for themselves. When Christians are on fire for God it is contagious, it leaves people asking, "What is your God like?" The amazing news is that you can find out for yourself.

Don't settle for religion when you can have relationship with Almighty God! Imagine the discernment and quality of decisions someone will make once they understand God in an intimate way!

It's exciting to me that we will never fully understand God, which means there is always something more we can learn and that He can reveal to us!

REFLECT: Do you know of God or do you know God? How would you describe your relationship with God to someone else? What aspect of your relationship with God would you change right now if you could? Pray and bring it before God.

Day 64

"The fear of the Lord is pure, enduring forever. The decrees
of the Lord are firm, and all of them are righteous. They
are more precious than gold, than much pure gold; they are
sweeter than honey, than honey from the honeycomb."
PSALMS 19:9-10 (NIV)

I worked in retail for many years and a common theme among customers who complained is that they did not believe the rules applied to them. Whether it was an expired coupon, returning an item past the warranty, or not wanting to wait in a line like everyone else, we often had people thinking that their situation was unique and required an exemption.

Now the rules in retail are written and stated; however, there is some flexibility to them. If someone explained their situation well and I have the authority to do so, I would usually help them out however I could. The difference was when someone demanded their way and told me what I have to do, then I would have much less motivation to help them out when they did not treat me with mutual respect.

I see people acting the same way with God. They demand Him to change the rules for them or they claim how certain parts of the Bible don't apply to them or their situation. Non-Christians may see the rules as archaic and irrelevant to today. Christians may see the rules as "suggestions" instead of things God has put in place for our own good.

The good news is that God is not a retail manager. He is a just and righteous judge. God is also full of grace that covers those in Jesus Christ. God is patient with us, wanting a relationship with His creation. Those who think we are only under grace and not obedience are missing the theme of the New Testament. Yes, we are not under the law as the law was never meant to save. Jesus did not come to abolish the law but to fulfill it. Following Jesus and letting the Holy Spirit change us will mean that we want to please God and follow the guidelines in the Bible.

The laws can be boiled down to love God and love others. There are also plenty of other warnings and directions we should heed when we are pursuing God fully but if you love God first, it is really hard to sin against Him.

Don't think you are an exception to God's plans and guidelines. Submit to God and He will direct your path. Discernment comes in not trying to change the rules but living by them as God intended and prioritizing a relationship with our Heavenly Father.

REFLECT: What do you or have you tried to be exempted from that the Bible commands? Do you submit to God and His plan for your life, or do you try to make things happen in your own effort? Submit to God today in prayer and express your desire for relationship with Him.

_____

_____

_____

_____

Day 65

*"Trust in the Lord with all your heart and lean not on
your own understanding; in all your ways submit to
him, and he will make your paths straight."*
PROVERBS 3:5-6 (NIV)

Valentine's Day is a commercialized holiday that couples
either celebrate or ignore. The holiday is symbolized by
hearts. You have hearts on décor, candy, greeting cards,
stuffed animals, boxes, and more. Giving a box of chocolates
to your love in the shape of a heart symbolizes that you are
giving your heart to them as well or that they already have
your heart.

Imagine if you gave your spouse a broken heart or candy in
the shape of half a heart? What if you could mathematically
calculate the amount of your romantic heart that your love
had and wrote that on a card? It might say something like,
Happy Valentine's Day to my wife that has 73% of my heart.
The rest of my heart is devoted to our kids, my parents, and
football... while that may be true, it sure isn't romantic!

I think Proverbs 3:5-6 is one of the best verses on discernment.
The entire process is laid out in one sentence. The process
starts with trusting in the Lord with all your heart. The
question then comes to mind, what does it mean to trust the
Lord with ALL your heart?

Trust implies confidence that something will function as intended or that someone will do what they say. If I didn't trust a chair, I wouldn't sit in it. If I didn't trust a bank, I wouldn't invest my money in it. If I didn't trust a babysitter, I wouldn't let her watch my kids. If I didn't trust a doctor, I definitely wouldn't let him or her perform surgery on me!

If we partially trust God, it is like getting one foot into the swimming pool. Fully trusting God is diving into the pool by believing fully that God is who He says He is.

God never changes, He never lies, and He never breaks a promise.

The promise that comes to us in this verse when we trust and submit is that our paths will be straight. Our decisions will be in line with what God wants us to do. Our future is in God's hands when we lay down our own pride and fear.

Trusting God never means that we know the future, but it does mean that our future is secure in the One who holds the universe together.

REFLECT: Would you say you trust God with all of your heart? What part of your life may you not be fully trusting God in? Give that to God today and ask Him to help make your paths straight going forward.

Day 66

"Husbands, love your wives, just as Christ loved the church and gave himself up for her to make her holy, cleansing her by the washing with water through the word, and to present her to himself as a radiant church, without stain or wrinkle or any other blemish, but holy and blameless."
EPHESIANS 5:25-27 (NIV)

Do you take only one shower or bath a year? I'm guessing (hoping) not. Why do we constantly have to take showers after we were clean? Even a child knows the answer to this... we get dirty again and again. There is also a personal preference at work in how much we like to be clean and how much we don't want to appear (smell) dirty to other people. If you care about each one of these, you are probably taking a shower every single day.

Ephesians talks about how Christ loved the church and gave Himself up for her to cleanse and wash her. He made the bride holy through His sacrifice on the cross, the free gift of grace that is nothing we can strive to achieve in our own efforts.

Not considering salvation anymore but sanctification, we are constantly getting polluted by the world and need cleansed by the Word of God. This may be caused by nothing more than living in the sinful world. If you go to work, hang out with friends, watch TV or scroll on social media, the filth of this world will try to attach itself to you. This spiritual dirt is what we need to cleanse ourselves of daily. It's a cleansing of our mind and thoughts.

There is also spiritual filth that we can personally sign up for when we sin. It is like a clean pig jumping right back into a muddy puddle. Even more so do we need to be cleansed again by the Holy Spirit and the Word of God. The problem comes when we are comfortable being spiritually dirty and when we don't care who smells us (aka a tarnished witness). If we are comfortable in sin, we may never want to be clean.

We must be transformed from looking like the filth of the flesh and this world. The living water of Jesus Christ is enough to cleanse us if we let it. When we are wallowing in dirt (sin), it is hard to make decisions and have discernment that leads us to clean (holy) outcomes.

If we stay relatively clean throughout the day, there is less work that we have to do in the shower. In the same way, if we keep ourselves free from sin and keep our eyes on Jesus daily, there will be less spiritual pollutants that we have to get rid of.

hink of taking your "spiritual shower" daily by taking
ne to pray, invest in reading the Word of God, and letting
conviction of the Holy Spirit clean you as the spotless
e of Christ.

ECT: What activities in your day do you feel
ually dirty" from and need to be cleaned? What are
vays you can take a "spiritual shower" daily and
the junk from the world?

Day 67

"The Lord God made garments of skin
for Adam and his wife and clothed them."
GENESIS 3:21 (NIV)

How do you react when you hear a child screaming in a retail store? Do you walk the other way? Do you give a nasty glance to the mom in hopes that she will get it together? Do you relate and think back to when your own kids did the same thing? Do you love someone else's child during their tantrum?

Whoa, you probably thought, "Of course I don't love someone else's kid!" Why don't you love them when they misbehave? Because you never loved them before that incident, and the~ are not your child. There is no relationship with a child ~ is a stranger.

When my kids act up it grieves me as a parent becau~ better for them. I want them to obey authority and ~ to punish them. I follow through with punish~ it is what is needed and will hopefully help ~ their mistakes. I always love my kids eve~ up... although I may not always like the~

If I have to take technology away fr~ I don't ignore him the rest of the ~ him, we might do a puzzle, Leg~

In the garden, Adam and Eve sinned and brought upon the punishment for all of humanity. God issued the punishment and Adam and Eve were both aware of their nakedness and shame. God made garments for them to cover and clothe them. This required an animal sacrifice. God has always provided the sacrifice. From Adam and Eve to Abraham and Isaac, and eventually Jesus Christ who was the perfect sacrifice for all of His children.

When discussing discernment and making decisions, it's important to understand that we will mess up and get it wrong. God does not reject us during this time. We may have to pay for the consequences of our actions, but God does not leave us to "figure it out" in our own strength.

We have to not let shame be a barrier between us and God. He is willing and able to guide us through the valleys in our life, even if we are responsible for getting to that point. Shame can cause us to run from God instead of running into His arms and asking for forgiveness from our heavenly Father.

REFLECT: What have been some negative consequences for your actions in the past and was God with you during those times? If you sin and make a mistake, how can you find comfort in God during times of discipline?

Day 68

"Then Zedekiah son of Kenaanah went up and slapped
Micaiah in the face. 'Which way did the spirit from the Lord
go when he went from me to speak to you?' he asked."
2 CHRONICLES 18:23 (NIV)

Some of the worst leaders I have worked with in the business world are those who have little confidence in their skills and abilities. They have to find their value in comparison to others and that usually involves trying to take them down in order to feel better about themselves. They are too busy gossiping or spreading division instead of actually focusing on getting work done and moving in one direction as a team.

Some of the best leaders are the complete opposite; confident, value teamwork, sees the value in other people's skills and abilities even if they are different from their own, and they stay focused on fixing problems instead of creating them.

I see a lot of similarities in the Christian church too when it comes to the calling God has placed on your life and how that compares with others. Those who are insecure and don't pursue a calling of their own, find pleasure in destroying the vision of others. They seek to gossip and spread lies instead of seeking God for themselves and focusing on a common goal.

The story in the verse in Chronicles with Michaiah is fascinating to me. Take some time to read the whole story. In short, there were a ton of false prophets who were telling the king what he wanted to hear and Michaiah was the only prophet who stood for what God was telling him. The other prophets were upset with him and instead of repenting, accused him of not hearing from God.

What God has asked you to do may not, and usually won't, make sense to someone else. No one is supposed to understand your calling. It was not a conference call when God gave it to you. But it is your responsibility to be faithful to that calling in obedience to God. Your calling is not usually a ten-year game plan from God, most of the times it will be a clear next step or He will ask you to be faithful where you are at.

Your discernment will falter if you listen to distractions or focus on other people instead of keeping your eyes on Jesus. People who have a rebellious spirit and a spirit of religion will love to make you a target when they see you taking ground for the Kingdom of God.

Stay faithful and God will reward your obedience with blessing.

REFLECT: What has God called you to do at this point of your life that is unique to you? What is a next step of faith you feel God has been showing you? Commit your faithfulness to God in prayer now.

_____

_____

_____

Day 69

*"Now Jesus loved Martha and her sister and Lazarus.
So when he heard that Lazarus was sick, he stayed where
he was two more days, and then he said to his disciples,
'Let us go back to Judea.'"*
JOHN 11:5-7 (NIV)

I hate flying, I'm not sure why exactly since the statistics on it show that it is very safe. Maybe I've watched one too many movies with a traumatic plane crash in them. There's something about being out of control and so far up in the sky that adds to the fear for me. To top that off, when I fly over the ocean it is even worse because of my fear of sharks!

What makes flying even worse is when there's a delay. Delays are never expected or planned for and they put a giant wrench in your plans. What was supposed to be a 3-hour trip could potentially be an all-day event with a huge layover.

When you have a flight that is delayed, what do you do? Do you give up on the trip? Do you forget about your vacation plans in Hawaii and spend the time in Nevada instead? More than likely you will continue with the plans you made. You have to get to the business meeting, the convention, the vacation because you have hotels booked, etc., and it's better to get there later than not at all. You do not abandon the trip.

Jesus delayed. After His friend Lazarus was sick, Jesus spent an extra two days where He was, much to the surprise of those around Him. Jesus said that it was part of the plan so that God would get the glory and the Son would be glorified through it. What looked like weakness and defeat ended up being a miraculous example of God's defeat over death.

Even when you have great discernment and are on the plan God has put before you, it will not always look the way you pictured. Delays and disappointments will come. There may be trials and difficulties. But will you continue to trust in God, or will you abandon the plan?

It's easy to get frustrated when we don't see the big picture. God tells you to start the ministry, but you don't get the funding. God tells you to foster children and they get taken away from you after you grow in love for them. God tells you to take the job only to work for a boss that is beyond frustrating.

Delay does not mean that you despair. Ask God for patient endurance through the delay and ask Him to use the delay for His glory.

REFLECT: What has God called you to do that had a delay in it even though it ended up working out? What are you going through right now that seems to have been delayed or put on hold? Ask God for wisdom in understanding His timing and for an increase in patience.

Day 70

"We hear that some among you are idle and disruptive.
They are not busy; they are busybodies. Such people
we command and urge in the Lord Jesus Christ to settle
down and earn the food they eat."
2 THESSALONIANS 3:11-12 (NIV)

As a father, I love giving my kids things that they enjoy. They may ask me for things like going miniature golfing or to a movie and, if the schedule works out, I will plan it because it brings them joy and I enjoy seeing them happy. They need me as a parent for this, they are not old enough to have the money or the transportation to get there themselves.

Now, on the other hand, if my kids asked me to clean their room, you can believe the answer would be, "Absolutely not, you are fully capable of cleaning your own room." One request required my provision and time. The other request was a misuse of my time, laziness on their part, and even a disbelief in their own abilities.

I believe we can ask anything from our Heavenly Father who loves to give good gifts to His children. However, we often ask for things that are fully within our capabilities and yet we want God to do all the work.

We might pray for revival without being willing to be a part of revival, we may pray for the homeless without being willing to feed them, we may pray for a job without being willing to apply and grow in our skills, we may pray for the church without being willing to serve in areas we are gifted in.

There's nothing wrong with praying for God to be with you along the journey and pray for discernment with decisions you will have to make. When I started blogging and having an online ministry, I had no clue how to blog or create a website. God gave me a noticeably clear and strong vision for the ministry and from there it was up to me to be the hands and feet to get it done. This required long hours of me researching all the skills of how to create a logo, a brand, a blog, a book, and even a podcast.

I love how 2 Thessalonians says that some in the church were idle and not busy but busybodies instead. Lazy Christians love to gossip and destroy other Christian's vision that God has given them without seeking God for themselves and having the fruit to show for their intimate relationship with God.

Don't ask God for what you are equipped and capable to do, instead ask Him for discernment along the way, provision in the process, and open doors that will help you quicken the journey.

REFLECT: What is a big thing you have asked God for that only He could provide? Did He? What is a small thing you asked God for that you were fully capable of? How would you pray differently after reading today's devotion?

"Then the Lord said to Cain, 'Why are you angry?
Why is your face downcast? If you do what is right,
will you not be accepted? But if you do not do what is
right, sin is crouching at your door; it desires to have
you, but you must rule over it.'"
GENESIS 4:6-7 (NIV)

I've always loved cats, I like dogs too but there's something about cats and their willpower, fierceness, and attitude that makes them a preferred favorite over dogs. I had lots of cats growing up, never more than one or two at a time. They were all outdoor cats, and we were in a desert so there was a ton of animals and reptiles that they would bring to the porch. The variety included things from birds, to lizards, to rabbits, and even a giant rat that was twice the size of the cat.

Cats love to play with their food. Not only do they like the chase but they like to torture their prey. One of my cats would catch a lizard and hold it down by the tail only to wait a couple minutes and release the lizard to start the chase over again.

When I think of crouching down, I think of cats. God gave Cain a pretty stern yet fair warning about sin. Cain was about to commit the second recorded sin by man and God, in His mercy, told Cain that sin was waiting to take a hold of him, crouching at his door, waiting to pounce.

Imagine if the sin at your door was like a kitten. Could you control a kitten that tried to attack you and enter your house? Of course, you might get a scratch, but you would win. Now imagine you fed that kitten, which was actually a lion cub. That lion cub grew into an adult. Now how hard would it be to stop that adult lion from entering your home? A lot harder!

We must rule over sin and that means that we do not feed it. We need to stop sin before it starts to get a hold of our life. Sin crouching at the door means it likes to stay hidden. Sin likes to work in secret and darkness. We must expose sin because darkness cannot hide in the light.

Unfortunately for Cain, even with a warning from God, it was not enough to stop sin in its tracks and take dominion over it. We have plenty of warnings in the Bible about what sin is and how to avoid it. We need to be smart and take dominion over the sin in our life with the power of the Holy Spirit.

REFLECT: What sin tends to lurk and crouch at the door of your life? How can you stop the sin before it grows and gets out of control? List the steps you can take to avoid mistakes that come when sin controls you.

_____

_____

_____

_____

Day 72

"But if you have doubts about whether or not you should eat something, you are sinning if you go ahead and do it. For you are not following your convictions. If you do anything you believe is not right, you are sinning."
ROMANS 14:23 (NLT)

Maybe you've been there, you post something on social media about a special time you are having with family or by yourself and out of nowhere BOOM, a Christian makes a comment about how you shouldn't be doing what you are doing. Maybe you shouldn't be celebrating a particular holiday, watching a particular movie, or drinking at a restaurant. How do you feel?

Social media has often replaced the church gossip that would critique people that came into the church for how they dressed, what they said, if they smoked, and if they had tattoos. I highly doubt if anyone responds to this type of loveless criticism with, "Wow, thank you for pointing that out, I will immediately change what I am doing."

The thing with convictions is that they are personal and cannot be passed around to others. In fact, those who try to pass their convictions onto others without love end up losing their audience and mostly likely their witness as Christians.

Think of that person who is on social media who is really into fitness. They post constantly about their workouts, before and after pictures, and their nicely portioned meals for the week. If you are not focusing on fitness, that person who posts this stuff is actually really annoying (they may be anyway even if you are into fitness). It's not that they are doing anything wrong, but they have convictions about fitness, and they are sharing it with others. When I see them focusing on fitness, I become all the more aware of how I am NOT focusing on working out or eating healthy. I then feel guilty for my workout habits and instead of changing, I simply dismiss or make fun of the fitness guru for their routine.

There are cut and dry sins in the Bible but unless the Holy Spirit does the work in someone's life, anyone, Christian or not, can justify their sin or just be apathetic toward it. Some convictions we have are on issues that the Bible is vague on. Not only that but depending on which denomination you are or which preacher you listen to, they may tell you to not worry about a particular sin because it is not relevant to today.

Let's take the person who smokes cigarettes for 10 years after being a Christian. In year 11, the Holy Spirit convicts them that smoking is not what is best for their body or their witness. Now if that person goes out and tells every other Christian that smokes that what they are doing is wrong, they are being a hypocrite! They did not care for 10 years no matter who told them and what research said it was bad for their health.

The things you are convicted about is between you and God. If, by chance, someone asks you why you believe what you believe or don't do what everyone else is doing, then that is your chance to speak truth with love into their life.

REFLECT: What things are you convicted about now that you were not convicted about in the past when you were a younger Christian? What things are you convicted today about that you would like to tell others to stop doing but shouldn't? Thank God for the convictions you have and ask Him to keep revealing new things to you.

Day 73

*"When you go through deep waters, I will be with you.
When you go through rivers of difficulty, you will not
drown. When you walk through the fire of oppression, you
will not be burned up; the flames will not consume you."*
ISAIAH 43:2 (NLT)

When I was young, I played soccer, nothing too competitive, but like most kids in grade school it was exercise. I was never great on offense, so I mostly played goalie. One game in particular was in the playoffs and our final placement to either get a trophy or not came down to a shootout. This was when each team took turns kicking the soccer ball at the goalie, one at a time. Now all of a sudden, my simple job became extremely important. We won the shootout and the game, and the trophy was ours. I had my ten seconds of feeling like a superstar MVP.

You've probably heard the saying, "The best offense is a good defense." In sports, you cannot afford to wait until the game starts to plan your defensive strategy, by then it will be too late.

When making decisions in life, you sometimes may feel like I did as goalie in the shootout, attack after attack coming after you due to no fault of your own. You may feel like you are constantly on the defense with decisions you are making. You did not choose the health problem, the unfaithful spouse, the betrayal at work, the slander from a church member, or the job loss.

Now there are times when the poor small decisions we make snowball into a bigger situation, but what I am discussing right now in today's devotional are situations that are completely out of your control.

How does discernment come into play when you did not decide to be put in the situation you are in? You play defense. You make the best decisions you can where you are at. You ask God for help navigating the troubled waters. As God promised Israel in Isaiah that He would be with them through deep waters, we can have the confidence that God will never leave us or forsake us.

Realize that no one decision you can make will make the problem you are in go away completely. It may be dozens of smaller decisions over time and with the peace and comfort of God along the way that will allow you to see breakthrough.

We cannot rely on discernment when life throws curve balls at us, but we can rely on God and make good decisions in the trials as God will lead us out of them.

REFLECT: What is an example of a stressful situation in your life that is happening or has happened due to no action of your own and it felt like you were playing defense? How can you rely on God's strength to get you through those times?

Day 74

"To those who sold doves he said, 'Get these out of here!
Stop turning my Father's house into a market!' His
disciples remembered that it is written:
'Zeal for your house will consume me.'"
JOHN 2:16-17 (NIV)

I managed a grocery store for many years. One customer complaint I remember vividly, and it was about a cake that was made for a party. It was not a kid's party, but it was a superhero party for adults. I'm not sure what exactly was in the party details, but the customer was extremely upset because the Wonder Woman cake that was made was "ruined" because the red orange in the border of the cake was the wrong shade of orange.

I offered to remake the cake which led to a larger conversation of how she wanted two cakes for one. The point of this story is her passion for a small detail in a cake was fascinating to me. How an entire party could be ruined over a small detail was either due to her passion for detail or projecting some other frustration upon the situation.

What I have realized over the years is how passionate people can be over things like hobbies, sports, cleaning, food, exercise, history, cars, etc. However, many Christians convey their faith with a "take it or leave it" mentality. They may not think about it, but their passion for Jesus is definitely not infectious to others looking at their life.

Even though I am not passionate about colors on a cake, I can understand what the customer many years ago was passionate about because we could not leave the conversation without at least me understanding where she was coming from.

As Christians, I believe we are called to be passionate about the things of God. Not every second of every day, but at the right time and in the right context. Jesus had zeal for the house of God that was evident to everyone the day he overturned tables at the temple.

When the time comes to express your faith, share your testimony, pray for someone, or love your neighbor, do you do it passionately? Our discernment that is fueled by zeal for God will allow us to be spirit led into situations where we can glorify God by our decisions. Personality does play into this, but I believe everyone can be passionate at the right times even if it is out of our comfort zone.

We can lose our passion for Jesus if we take our eyes off of Him. When others see you looking at Jesus, they will gaze in that same direction. It's similar to that social experiment where one or two people are looking up at nothing in the sky to see how many random people walking by will look up too. Keep looking up!

Reflect: Is your faith passionately infectious to those around you? How would someone else describe your faith? Ask God for a fresh fire of the Holy Spirit that will lead you into decisions and conversations with passion!

Day 75

"On hearing this, Jesus said to them, 'It is not the healthy who need a doctor, but the sick. I have not come to call the righteous, but sinners.'"
MARK 2:17 (NIV)

Several years ago, I went in to see the doctor. I had received a diagnosis that was troubling, but I wanted a second opinion. I pursued various tests and doctors to confirm what was previously said and also in hope that the first doctor was wrong, everything turned out to be OK but caused me to think.

I find it interesting that when I go see the doctor for physicals or other reasons, if the doctor says that everything is ok, I'm thinking, "Awesome, see you next time!" Why don't I get a second opinion when I receive good news? It's probably because I'm be afraid the second doctor would find something that was missed so it's just best to stay away.

The correlation can be made with the church today. People love to hear a "good diagnosis." People don't feel the need to seek out someone else when preachers tell us things like: "we are awesome", "God loves us no matter what we do", "the sin called out in Bible doesn't apply to today", "God wants you to be prosperous and wealthy!" We walk away feeling good about ourselves from these messages as a type of "if it ain't broke don't fix it" mentality. There's nothing wrong with feeling positive, but the problem arises when the tables turn and we start to hear messages about sin or something that is trying to motivate us to change a behavior. What is our response to that?

Jesus said in Mark 2:17 that He has not come to call the righteous but sinners. I almost feel like Jesus is referring to the righteous here as "righteous" with finger quotes. The Pharisees at the time could not understand why Jesus was with the tax collectors and other sinners. These "sinners" were actually willing to listen to Jesus. The Pharisees were too busy in their self-righteousness to realize that they needed a Savior too!

A part of having discernment is being able to see if the message we hear aligns with the Bible and how it applies to our life. If a message being preached or advice a friend has for us, does in fact align with the Bible, we have an obligation to take it to heart and act upon it.

REFLECT: How can I do a better job of applying wisdom I hear to my life? Am I currently listening to sound doctrine and have I sought out the Bible for myself to verify?

Day 76

"The heart is deceitful above all things,
and desperately wicked; Who can know it?"
JEREMIAH 17:9 (NKJV)

Unfortunately, I ended up seeing a lot of romantic comedy movies in the late 90's and early 2000s. It was sort of expected of me since this was the time when I was dating. They were not all terrible movies, but they were cliché and an unrealistic portrayal of love. The point of these "Rom-Com" movies was not to be a documentary, but to be entertaining.

The women in the movies usually had to make some drastic choice by the end. They had some realization that the person they wanted all along was not the one that everyone else thought they should be interested in. The woman left high society to fall for the guy from nowhere. Another woman left a movie career to be with a simple bookstore owner. And another would leave her current boyfriend to reunite with a guy from 10 years ago because it was just serendipity!

The common theme of these "Rom-Coms" was to "follow your heart" in romantic relationships. In fact, following your heart is a common decision-making strategy for many people and not just in romance.

The heart, however, is a terrible source of discernment. Jeremiah says the heart is deceitfully wicked, who can know it? For the Christian, our sources of discernment should be the Bible, Holy Spirit, and godly relationships. If your heart leads you away from Jesus, it's not the path you are supposed to be on... bottom line.

When we are aligned with Jesus, His desires will become our desires. When we keep our eyes on Jesus, we will only want what the Father wants. Jesus even said, "Yet not my will but yours be done" (Luke 22:42) when He was in the garden and His human desires did not want to go to the cross.

But you might hear "the heart wants what the heart wants" as if that is an excuse to make a poor or hurtful decision. As Christians, we are called to die to self! Is this what the heart wants? Absolutely not!

Jesus cannot be Lord of your life if He is not Lord of your heart. Your heart will get you in trouble if it is not brought into alignment with the will of God and the Word of God.

REFLECT: What has your heart wanted that you knew was not God's will for your life? What does your heart desire today? Write down things that you desire in your flesh and also in your spirit and look at the differences between them.

_____

_____

_____

_____

_____

Day 77

"Good planning and hard work lead to prosperity,
but hasty shortcuts lead to poverty."
PROVERBS 21:5 (NLT)

One of the major differences between a good and bad employee, I have found, is how they utilize their time while they are at work. Having managed many employees in a retail setting, I was able to see plenty of *poor examples* of how time could be *mismanaged*. What really was frustrating is the excuses. Whenever someone would say, "I didn't have time to complete my work," I could usually help them remember times in the day when they were not using their time wisely.

Sometimes a lazy employee would take a longer break than was allowed, they might socialize too much, not work with a sense of urgency, or not utilize their down time efficiently. After all, if you have time to lean, you have time to clean I would always say!

For every action we make with our time, there is an opportunity cost associated with it. This is the cost of choosing one thing over another. For example, if I spend two hours watching a movie, that is two hours I cannot spend in doing something else. We cannot add to our allotted time in a day, but we can be more efficient with our time.

If you say, "I do not have time for something" that is somewhat of a false statement. A more correct statement would be "I am not making time for that." My Mom would always say, "We make time in life for the things that are important to us."

If you say God is at the top of your priorities, how does that reflect in how you spend your day? Maybe you need to create a better schedule and stick to it. Free time is necessary but it's important to know how much free time you have and not use time that you should be spending on something else for things that are ultimately frivolous.

For example, if I spend eight hours playing video games when I have things to get done around the house, projects to complete at work, and I did not spend any time with my wife or kids, that eight hours of video games was poorly used time!

No one on their death bed wishes they spent more time on social media or watching movies. We need to have discernment with our time and give value to the things that are the most important in life.

REFLECT: How can you have better discernment with the time that you have during the day? What frivolous activities get in the way of things you say are important to you? How much is social media eating away at your time and stealing your peace?

_____

_____

_____

_____

Day 78

"But if serving the Lord *seems undesirable to you, then choose for yourselves this day whom you will serve, whether the gods your ancestors served beyond the Euphrates, or the gods of the Amorites, in whose land you are living. But as for me and my household, we will serve the* Lord.*"*
JOSHUA 24:15 (NIV)

What is your favorite ice cream flavor? For me, we must go back to my early years when I was around 6 years old, and my parents would take me to K-Mart. We would get ice cream there when we went shopping and one flavor I would always get is Superman ice cream. Sure, it may just be nostalgia, but I would still rate this as my favorite flavor. Also, they still make this flavor, but I only know of one place in my state where you can find it.

Unfortunately, many people treat Jesus like an ice cream flavor. They "try" Jesus and if they don't like what they hear or don't like how other Christians represent Him, they reject Him and move on to a flavor they like. The major problem with that is that Jesus is Lord, even though we have free will, there is really only one correct option in life.

Unfortunately, there are many churches that do not represent the biblical Jesus and many people feel that if they tried church, they tried Jesus. Jesus is a commitment, not an experiment. We should dedicate our life to being changed by the Holy Spirit and to be more like Him.

Once you become a Christian, living for Jesus is not like a custom ice cream store where you can pick the toppings, candy, syrups, and ice cream that you want. It's all or nothing. We have to stay true to the full Word of God and our obedience to it.

Not cherry-picking the Bible is an important component in discernment. When we make decisions in areas where we have not fully submitted to God, it leads to sin and negative consequences. The message of the Gospel is designed for all; however it is not designed to fit your flesh.

Joshua made the commitment for him and his family to serve the Lord. Even though there were other options he could have chosen, in his mind there was only one. He made a public commitment for others to see and was faithful to that choice.

Will you make that commitment today?

REFLECT: What areas of the Bible do you see Christians today choose to discard? What parts of following Christ do you not want to do in your flesh but you know you need to? Write them all down and pray over each one, asking God to give you strength to stay focused on Him.

_____

_____

_____

_____

Day 79

"So Abimelek summoned Isaac and said, 'She is really your wife! Why did you say, 'She is my sister'?' Isaac answered him, 'Because I thought I might lose my life on account of her.'"
GENESIS 26:9 (NIV)

As a parent, I face a frequent realization that I sound like my parents did when I did not want to listen to them. Once, I told my son who complained about dinner, "Remember there are kids around the world who would love to be eating what you are eating right now!" I also felt the need to educate my kids on movies and music from my childhood and realized this must be what it was like when my parents educated me on movies and music from the 1950s!

For me, I had great parents so it's not that I am sad for sounding like them. I think it's more the mental realization that I am no longer as young as I once was. If you are like me your brain thinks you are 10-15 years younger than you really are and your body feels like it's 10 years older than it really is!

It's natural for parents to want to pass on their knowledge and interests to their kids but sounding like them also gives you an awareness when you do some of the negative things they did too. You may have thought, "Ugh, I swore I would never become my father," and here you are fighting some of the same vices.

I'm sure Isaac could relate too. In our verse today, he is in Genesis doing the same thing to his wife that Abraham did. Both were too fearful to trust in God that they lied to the king that their wife was their sister. I can imagine Isaac grew up and heard about this story and maybe even heard his dad joke about it. Yet when Isaac's merit needed testing, he fell into the same trap his dad did because it's "what he knew."

What we know and how we were raised is not an excuse for poor decision making and sinful behavior. We all start somewhere; we have influences into our lives from the personality God gave us and examples we were shown. Nature vs. nurture. It takes discernment to know what we are prone to do, how we react to things, what sins we have because it's what we've seen or been exposed to, and what the general direction our personality will lean us toward.

It doesn't matter if you had a great or poor childhood, we all take baggage from our childhood that needs to be left at the foot of the cross. It doesn't mean we forget about the past and become a different person, but we focus on the good things we learned and identify challenges we are prone to facing and let the Holy Spirit change you from within.

Also, even if you had a really poor childhood or a nonexistent parent, God can redeem your story, it's sort of His thing. I would even believe there are plenty of good lessons you learned along the way even if it is your tendency to paint your story with a broad negative brush. God can use your story and make it His Story!

REFLECT: List some positive and negative influences from your childhood and tendencies from your personality that you have. Review the negative ones, how can you not be influenced by them and let the Holy Spirit change you to not succumb to them?

Day 80

*"Do not be anxious about anything, but in every
situation, by prayer and petition, with thanksgiving,
present your requests to God. And the peace of God,
which transcends all understanding, will guard your
hearts and your minds in Christ Jesus."*
PHILIPPIANS 4:6-7 (NIV)

My wife and I dealt with a situation where there were thick
white layers of dust that were accumulating all over our
daughter's room. It was on the fan, bookshelves, picture
frames, and even her stuffed animals. Whenever we would
clean the room, the thick white dust would appear within
a week or two. We were frustrated in trying to figure out the
cause, as this was the only room in the house to experience this
and we were genuinely concerned for our daughter's health.

We called air conditioner and air quality companies, but they
did not know why that was the only room in the house affected
by the white dust. We even considered a restructuring of
our air condition vents that would have cost thousands of
dollars in hopes that the air flow was the culprit.

As it turns out, we learned that the humidifier we had was
an ultrasonic humidifier which required distilled water. We
were using regular tap water which was causing the minerals
in the water to be released into the air. A long and frustrating
problem was solved with a remarkably simple fix!

This caused me to think how many problems in our lives often seem incredibly stressful and we lack peace in trying to solve them. We may seek very advanced solutions that the world has to offer while missing a quite simple component that will fix the problem.

To be honest, if I read and followed the instructions on the humidifier, I would have never had the problem with the white dust.

Many people miss out on very simple instructions in the Bible. It's easy to think, "that's too simple" or "it can't be that easy," but we miss out on the fact that sometimes the most complicated problems require simple solutions.

If your life seems to be out of control, or maybe a day is out of control, don't go to an extreme solution. The Bible calls us to do simple things and do them often. Pray. Trust. Fast. Rejoice. Love. Ask for discernment.

Maybe your giant problem will be easily resolved when you let go and let God do what He does best. The Bible tells us that when we present our requests to God, peace will flow, peace that passes all understanding from the Prince of Peace.

REFLECT: What are some simple things that the Bible commands that you can do during the day? What is a giant problem in your life that you thought required drastic action but in reality only required simple obedience and trusting God?

Day 81

"Keep your lives free from the love of money and be content with what you have, because God has said, 'Never will I leave you; never will I forsake you.'"
HEBREWS 13:5 (NIV)

When it's around the time to buy a new car, I sometimes spend months researching and being anxious about the idea. Buying a new car becomes this goal that needs to be reached at all costs. I make sure I research the differences between models, the price ranges between years, and how much the financed amount will cost monthly. I will spend hours searching on the Internet for good deals, frequently checking used cars sites for restocking.

In my search for a car, I may reach out to a dealer and test drive the car. I may let a salesperson know what car I am in the market for so they can keep an eye out for me. I will be on the lookout for deals such as zero percent financing or cash back.

Finally, when I buy a car, my search is complete. I enjoy driving it home, I take some pictures to share, and that's it, I am content... or I should be. You see the thing with things is that things cannot satisfy you. They may for a moment or a bunch of moments, but eventually that new car, new house, new boat, or new toy won't be new anymore and you will be on to the next thing. This is nothing new in the human condition.

There's nothing wrong with things. There's nothing wrong with relationships or jobs either. The problem becomes when we rely on these things to bring us lasting contentment when our true contentment should be in God first.

The Bible commands us to be free from the love of money which becomes an idol if we let it, just like anything can become an idol if it takes priority over God in our life.

We will all need to buy new things like a car or a house, however the trick is to realize what need they will fulfill. A new house will not change your struggling marriage. A new car will not fill the longing in your soul for a relationship with your Creator.

If our longing for something other than God is greater than our longing for God, then there's a problem. If Jesus is not enough, nothing else ever will be.

REFLECT: What is something you thought would bring you contentment but didn't? What are some ways you can remind yourself to be content with what you have first? Take time to thank God that He will never leave or forsake you.

_____

_____

_____

_____

_____

Day 82

"Those who belong to Christ Jesus have nailed the passions and desires of their sinful nature to his cross and crucified them there. Since we are living by the Spirit, let us follow the Spirit's leading in every part of our lives."
GALATIANS 5:24-25 (NLT)

I remember very little about Driver Education class in high school, but I do remember two things. First, we were shown an extremely old instructional video that was probably 30-40 years old at the time. The man in the car would drive overly slow through a town that looked like it was in the 1950s and wave at everyone and honk if there was any chance that a car was coming in his general vicinity, a courtesy honk if you will. He would also wait after a green light for about 20 seconds, just to make sure that no one was coming. Imagine if someone did that today?

The other thing I remember is that I got an easy question wrong on a test. The question had a true/false response to the question: "You make constant adjustments to the steering wheel while you drive?" I didn't have much practice driving at the time and the question confused me, so I answered false. Sometimes when I drive now, I am consciously aware of how much I make adjustments on the steering wheel even if I'm driving on a straight road.

Paul told the church in Galatia to "follow the Spirit's leading in every part of our lives," this should be constant adjustments in our spirit by the leading of the Holy Spirit as we travel down the road of life.

Passions and desires of the sinful nature don't go away, but we nail them to the cross, meaning we give them up. We don't seek after them; we need to die to them daily. It doesn't mean the desires always go away, sometimes they do, other times we have to overcome them.

We need discernment every day as we make decisions that can either have a positive or negative effect on our lives and those around us. The problem comes when we try to do everything in our own power and we try to get through the day, through a crisis, through a relationship issue, or through a financial setback in our own strength.

Allow the Holy Spirit to make adjustments for you on the decisions you make daily. This requires an intimate relationship with God and the ability to quiet all the other influences that may try to steer you away from your purpose and calling.

REFLECT: What are some of the passions and desires of your sinful nature that you need to nail on the cross daily? What are some daily decisions that you make that you need the help of the Holy Spirit with?

_____

_____

_____

_____

Day 83

"Then the Lord said to Abraham, 'Why did Sarah laugh?
Why did she say, 'Can an old woman like me have
a baby?' Is anything too hard for the Lord? I will return
about this time next year, and Sarah will have a son.'"
Genesis 18:13-14 (NLT)

At my retail job that I had for many years, one holiday season we got word of a change coming from corporate. This change was huge, it was one of the biggest changes in how we structure our processes to happen in the last couple decades. Our district got the not-so-brilliant idea of implementing it right away, right before Christmas, and before there was a clear and succinct strategy from headquarters rolled out to all stores.

In short, this rollout was a complete disaster. We were essentially the self-inflicted guinea pigs for this rollout. We tried and failed, adjusted, and pivoted constantly. It was the worse time of year to change something so significant without a clear strategy and it was, without a doubt, the worst holiday season in my twenty plus years at the company.

About a year later, the plan rolled out to the entire company in a well formatted and supported way that allowed stores to be successful. There were still challenges, but not at the level as when we tried to muscle it through on our own.

I think this is sometimes how we are as Christians, God gives us a vision, a glimpse at where He is taking us and we want make it happen now!

Look at Isaac and Sarah, God said Abraham would have descendants as vast as the stars in the sky and it was impossible for them to believe that as they were without children and Sarah was barren. They even tried to take matters into their own hands and make God's word come to pass in their own timing and thus birthed Ishmael. It wasn't until Isaac was born that the fulfillment of what they knew years ago came to pass.

The things that God gives you a vision for may be weeks or even years down the road. You cannot sledgehammer open a door in trying to make it happen in your own efforts, otherwise it is up to you to keep that door open in your own strength and not by the power of God.

Maybe you are desperate to get married that you are forcing a relationship that is not honoring God to happen. Maybe you are stuck at a job that you don't like and you are looking at options that are not from God in order to get away from it. Maybe you are desperate for a child and you are not finding contentment with what God has given you in the moment. I've been in all three of these scenarios, by the way.

Patience is key, God's timing is best. Waiting on the Lord is not easy but it is worth it in the long run.

REFLECT: In what ways have you tried to take the vision and plan God has given you into your own hands? What things are you discontented with in your life that you want to change? What is a small step that God is leading you in today in order to move toward a vision He has given you? Pray about it if you are unsure.

"Let the word of Christ dwell in you richly in all wisdom, teaching and admonishing one another in psalms and hymns and spiritual songs, singing with grace in your hearts to the Lord."
COLOSSIANS 3:16 (NKJV)

I think most people have an era of movies and specific genres that they grew up watching that they could quote instantly in the right moment. Something triggers memory of a scene or a phrase and you finish it with a movie quote for all to hear around you whether they get the reference or not. Maybe that's just me. My go to quotes are usually '90s comedies, John Wayne, and Laurel & Hardy movies because those are what I watched the most.

There was also a movie that I would watch as a kid over and over again. Sometimes I would watch it and immediately put it (the VCR tape) back in to watch a second time. My kids as well will seem to have a movie of the week or month where that is all they want to watch until they finally get tired of it. My wife and I get tired of it about the second time!

How can you quote favorite movies of yours with such ease? Because of repetition! You have seen them so much that they become ingrained in your memory. Also, you usually enjoy them. The same is with the Word of God. Not only is it truth and our foundation but it is living and active. You should enjoy reading the Word and realize that many around the world would love to be able to have access to read it themselves.

The more you read the Bible, the more you get the Bible in you. This means that you can recall verses by memory, or the Holy Spirit can quicken them to you as you need them. Our number one source of discernment as Christians is the Bible. It would be a shame if we neglected it because of the excuse that we have read it before, and we have nothing new to learn.

When I was younger, I was able to memorize the longest Psalm, Psalm 119. This was quite the feat but honestly didn't stay in my brain for very long after.

It's truly not just how much Scripture you know, it's how much Scripture you live. Even atheists have read the Bible, and some know it better than Christians. The difference is application and faith in believing it to be the Word of God.

REFLECT: What does your daily routine look like to read the Word of God? Do you find yourself applying what you read and meditating on the Word? Thank God that you have access to His Word today!

Day 85

"So, my dear brothers and sisters, be strong and
immovable. Always work enthusiastically for the Lord, for
you know that nothing you do for the Lord is ever useless."
1 CORINTHIANS 16:58 (NLT)

Who is that person at your church that always has a smile?
Who is the person at your church that serves in every
capacity possible and is there no matter what is happening?
There are usually these people in every church. They are
not usually paid and yet they give of their time and talent
to further the Kingdom of God, why?

I've heard it estimated that twenty percent of the people in
churches do eighty percent of the work. What would it look
like if every person stepped up and into a role that furthered
the mission of the church? What would the church be able
to do financially if every single person gave ten percent?

Two of my close friends started a ministry from a need they
saw in the community. They noticed that for people that
needed lawns mowed, cars fixed, air conditioners worked on,
paint jobs completed, etc., the church should step up in this
role and serve. They did not wait for someone to do it, they
had the skill and with the blessing of the church leadership,
they started the ministry. They did not do it for the clout, the
money, and definitely not because they had a lot of free time.
They had a heart for serving as unto the Lord.

I am not trying to convict you to do more than you are currently doing. I want the connection between what the Bible says and your heart. Paul tells the church in Corinth that nothing they do for the Lord is ever useless and to do all things enthusiastically for the Lord. Everyone has a bad day but if you look beat up and distraught all the time, people may wonder what is so special about this God you serve if you look like everyone else.

How does serving God keep our eyes on Jesus? Because our eyes are off of ourselves! Serving others is the best way to keep from focusing on your own problems and what you have or do not have. No task is too small for the kingdom. People like to highlight certain roles in ministry as being more important than others, however if you are doing it for God it is important to God.

Not everyone is called to be a pastor or an elder, but everyone is called to love their neighbor. If God is highlighting a passion or a need in the church or an area of influence, it could be that He has plans for YOU to fill that need!

REFLECT: Do you make the connection that God values even the smallest thing you do for Him? Do you work enthusiastically for God or do people hear you complain? Pray and ask God that you will always keep your eyes on Jesus as you are doing things for Jesus.

Day 86

"The tongue has the power of life and death,
and those who love it will eat its fruit."
PROVERBS 18:21 (NIV)

The moment you hit send on an email and instantly regret it is not a good feeling! If you are like me, you have constructed many emails or text messages and deleted them when you either reread them or asked for feedback.

One time at work, I sent an email response to someone that was accusing me of something in a passive aggressive way. I felt the need to defend myself, so I formulated a specific response to show how I was in the right and copied a couple of my managers in on the conversation. As soon as I sent the email, I regretted it but there wasn't much I could do. One of my bosses responded with, "Next time just pick up the phone and call them to figure this out."

We must have discernment daily with our words, whether spoken or written. I always tell my son, "When you say something you can't put the words back in your mouth. Sometimes the damage you do can be fixed with an apology and other times it cannot." The Bible is abundantly clear on the power of our words and the tongue, just read the book of James.

Many times, we speak out of strong emotions like anger, fear, and pride. Using discernment allows us to think outside of those emotions; if we would not be proud of saying something later on after the emotions have subsided, we should show restraint.

The power of our words is not only in doing damage but also in speaking a blessing. Giving someone a kind word, praying over your children, or expressing love for your spouse are all ways in which our words can be used to speak life and not death.

A good rule of thumb is to not speak your first response in a difficult or heated situation. Take time, pray, and ask for wisdom from others before you construct a response. This can be hard in situations that seem to demand a response from you immediately, but it is wisdom to not let the moment overpower your ability to seek God.

REFLECT: What are some situations you find yourself in where it is hard to craft a loving response to someone? What are some practical steps you can take in order to calm down and pray before giving in to the emotions of the moment? If you have time, read James Chapter 3 as a final reflection on this topic for today.

_____

_____

_____

_____

_____

Day 87

"Rescue others by snatching them from the flames of judgment. Show mercy to still others, but do so with great caution, hating the sins that contaminate their lives."
JUDE 1:23 (NLT)

Have you ever worked on commission or been motivated at work because of a special project or sales goal? When I was a young manager, we had a sales competition over four categories of items we were trying to sell at a retail store. The competition was among twelve stores total with four total prizes. We had a month to drive as many sales for these four categories as possible.

I took the challenge with enthusiasm. I did everything in my power to promote these categories to customers in the store. I made sure the areas were clean and clutter free. I came up with special promotions. I experimented with placement and verbiage used to draw in people. By the end of the competition, I won 3 of the 4 sales contests.

Sometimes success is a matter of motivation. As Christians, we often lack the motivation to share the Gospel of Jesus Christ with others. There are many reasons for this: fear, not knowing what to say, assuming they have already heard it, not loving them enough, thinking someone else will do it, etc. I've been guilty of all of these.

Now, hypothetically speaking, I will present a terrible idea to you... Ready? What if our job was commission based and required us to preach the Gospel to as many people as possible? What if our very livelihood in our income was determined by how many people we spoke to about Jesus in a given day? Do you think we would be more motivated? I would guess so.

Jesus gave the Great Commission to go and make disciples of all nations (Matt 28:19), this should be motivation enough because our Lord and Savior commanded it! Not only that but as Jude says, we have to see those who don't know Jesus as needing to be snatched from the fire. There is a lot at stake, and we cannot be lazy in this endeavor. We have to be diligent and wise, using discernment as to when and where to share our faith.

What does evangelism have to do with making wise decisions and keeping our eyes on Jesus? A lot! If our eyes are not on ourselves, but on those who need to be shown love, we are not focused on being self-centered and absorbed in our own problems. Our desires shift in becoming God's desires for the lost.

This world gives no hope, it's easy to forget what it is like to not have Christ when we become Christian, but we have what others want, even if they do not realize it yet. We should share with boldness knowing that they face an eternity apart from Christ.

REFLECT: Be honest between you and God: What are some reasons you do not share the Gospel as much as you would like? What are some ways you can improve in your confidence in sharing the Gospel? Write down three people who need to hear about Jesus that you know and pray for them.

_____

_____

_____

"But Lot's wife looked back, and she became a pillar of salt."
GENESIS 19:26 (NIV)

I have an app that I check daily that tells me what I posted on that day across various social media sites. All types of content are displayed from a year ago to over ten now. I can look back on pictures of my kids when they were younger, a family trip we took, a frustrating day I had, and more. I'm sometimes embarrassed by what I wrote many years ago before I had better discernment on social media.

The thing with looking back is that it can fill you with a mix of emotions, not always good. If you look back on a phase of your life when you were happier, you might be discontented. If an old picture jogs a memory of a previous relationship, you might be discontented with your spouse. If you see a different job you had, you might be discontented with your job.

Lot's wife looked back and she was destroyed because of it. Two angels came to Sodom and Gomorrah to get Lot's family out of there before fire and brimstone rained down on it. Lot's sons-in-law thought Lot was joking when he warned them. Lot and his wife and their two daughters hesitated, and the two angels had to grab them by the hand to lead them to safety. The Bible says this was the Lord's mercy that they were pulled out of that city (Genesis 19:16 NIV).

Even with the mercy of God and a warning not to look back, Lot's wife did. She just needed to see what was happening and possibly longed to be back in a city that was filled with debauchery and licentiousness. Jesus even warned His disciples to, "Remember Lot's wife!" (Luke 17:32 NIV).

There's nothing wrong with reminiscing on the past, but when you start to long for the sin God pulled you out from and when you take for granted the mercy God is showing you, it becomes a problem. We cannot have discernment when we do not see what is in front of us but compare our current circumstance with the past.

Watch for the triggers you might have when you start to engage with thoughts that lead you away from the blessings you have today. Our enemy loves to bring discontentment into our lives and we need to ultimately be content with God and God alone.

REFLECT: What are some things God has saved you from that you should never go back to? What are some thoughts you have to fight about returning to things that are not good for your spirit? What things can you thank God for today that are in front of you and ahead of you?

Day 89

"My son, pay attention to what I say; turn your ear to my words. Do not let them out of your sight, keep them within your heart; for they are life to those who find them and health to one's whole body. Above all else, guard your heart, for everything you do flows from it."
PROVERBS 4:20-23

I like to ask people I talk to on my podcast, "If you could meet anyone alive or dead, except Jesus who is alive, who would it be?" There is a wide range of people that are chosen as a response to that question. They range from Bible characters, presidents, actors, musicians, authors, and more!

One of the most interesting answers to this question of who you would like to meet was from a guy who said, "Myself, ten years ago." He wanted to be able to stop himself from making mistakes that could have been avoided if they just had a little more knowledge. He wasn't talking about sharing lottery numbers or winning sports teams with his younger self, but wisdom into who he could be if he pursued the right things in life.

I'm sure we would all love to be in a position of being able to share wisdom with a younger version of ourselves. That is why so many parents are so passionate in their instructions to their children, they want their kids to be able to avoid as many problems that they had as possible.

King Solomon thought the same thing, much of the first part of the book of Proverbs is him telling "his son" wisdom on what to do and what not to do. Solomon, with as much wisdom as God gave him, still made many poor decisions especially concerning women.

We only have one shot in life to get it right, and we will fail in many ways. Since we can never time travel back to correct our mistakes, it is wisdom to listen to those who have gone ahead of us and who have wisdom beyond our years.

Asking for help and advice is a sign of strength, not weakness. I always knew when I was training someone at work whether they had good or bad potential just in the way they listened and engaged during their training. If they acted like they knew everything and didn't ask questions, I did not give them very long to last at the job.

No matter what stage in life you are at, we are always learning, however our motivation might be lower than it was before. God has given us the Bible that is filled with more wisdom than we can fully understand in our life, and yet there are principles that are there for our good if we would just apply them.

REFLECT: What would you tell yourself ten years ago? What do you think you would stay to yourself ten years from now?

_____

_____

_____

_____

Day 90

"Let us hold tightly without wavering to the hope we affirm, for God can be trusted to keep his promise. Let us think of ways to motivate one another to acts of love and good works."
HEBREWS 10:23-24 (NLT)

Who was your favorite sports coach? How about favorite teacher? More than likely your favorite was not only knowledgeable, but they were motivational. You wanted to be around them and most likely they helped you during a pivotal time in your life.

My favorite teacher was my high school math teacher. He was smart, funny, and genuinely cared for his students. He didn't give us a free pass for grades, but you could tell that he wanted everyone to be successful. He constantly found new ways to motivate his students.

If you are the only person around with your eyes on Jesus is that ok with you? It shouldn't be. Even if your eternity is secure, you should have a passion for those that may not know Jesus or those who just need some motivation in staying close to Him.

We are encouraged in Hebrews to think of ways to motivate each other. To think of ways means cultivating the action based on our audience. What will motivate one person may not motivate the other.

Some people have the gift of encouragement, it comes effortlessly. Even if encouraging people does not come naturally to you, you may need to be more strategic about it. Sometimes I will set a calendar reminder weekly or monthly to reach out to a certain person. I might mimic a good idea I saw someone else doing.

You influence people in one way or another. There may be someone that has their eyes off Jesus who needs a loving nudge in the right direction. If someone keeps their eyes off Jesus for too long it can lead to devastating effects.

It's important to remember that no one can be forced to keep their eyes on Jesus. You cannot turn someone's head or pry their eyes open towards Jesus. Just like when we witness to unbelievers, we can only plant the seeds and let the Holy Spirit do the work. If someone is stuck in sin, they do not need more condemnation, they may already feel the conviction if the Holy Spirit is inside them.

Ultimately, one of the best ways to encourage someone to keep their eyes on Jesus is to model it. Let your passion for Jesus spark a fire in others. Let others see how your focus on Jesus gives you hope when others are hopeless and show love when others show hate.

When having your eyes on Jesus turns into a heart change, that's when the power of the Gospel comes to life!

REFLECT: Are you concerned for those around you that may need encouragement in keeping their eyes on Jesus? Who can you encourage and motivate today out of love? Pray, then send them a message of encouragement.